Censorship in Schools

Victoria Sherrow

—Issues in Focus—

Enslow Publishers, Inc.

44 Fadem Road   PO Box 38
Box 699   Aldershot
Springfield, NJ 07081   Hants GU12 6BP
USA   UK

Copyright © 1996 by Victoria Sherrow

Library of Congress Cataloging-In-Publication Data

Sherrow, Victoria.
   Censorship in schools / Victoria Sherrow.
      p. cm. — (Issues in focus)
   Includes bibliographical references (p.   ) and index.
   Summary: Discusses issues surrounding various types of censorship which occur
in schools including censorship of literature, courses, textbooks, and expression.
   ISBN 0-89490-728-X
   1. Academic freedom—United States—Juvenile literature. 2. Public
schools—Censorship—United States—Juvenile literature. [1. Censorship.
2. Schools.] I. Title. II. Series: Issues in focus (Hillside, N.J.)
LC72.2.S54 1996
025.213—dc20   96-14470
                                          CIP
                                          AC

Printed in the United States of America

10 9 8 7 6 5 4 3 2 1

Photo Credits: AP/Wide World Photos, p. 7; The Bettmann Archive,
p. 66; Collection of the Supreme Court of the United States, p. 97;
Deborah J. Dwyer, p. 105; Harris & Ewing, Collection of the Supreme
Court of the United States, p. 96; Jeffrey Sobiech, The Mark Twain House,
p. 107; Joseph Conn/*Church & State*, pp. 18, 23, 109; Library of Congress,
pp. 9, 33, 35; The Mark Twain House, p. 42; The Metropolitan Museum
of Art, Wolfe Fund, 1931. Catharine Lorillard Wolfe Collection, p. 26;
Mick Pauli, 58; National Archives, p, 75; National Geographic Society,
Collection of the Supreme Court of the United States, p. 69; National Park
Service, p. 31; Photo/Courtesy of *The Des Moines Register*, p. 94;
Reproduced with permission of Harcourt Brace & Company, Canada,
p. 72; UPI/Bettmann, p. 68; Victoria Sherrow, p. 46.

Cover Photo: © Rob Nelson, 1990, Black Star, PNI

Contents

1

Conflicts in the Schools

In 1994, teachers at a high school in Mifflinburg, Pennsylvania, cancelled two field trips. Students had been scheduled to see Shakespeare's play *Macbeth* and a free screening of Steven Spielberg's film *Schindler's List,* which shows Nazi atrocities toward Jews and others during World War II. Some local citizens called them unsuitable for young people.

That same year, in Lancaster, Pennsylvania, citizens objected to students viewing *A Thousand Cranes.* In this play, a Japanese girl dies from radiation sickness, after the atomic bombing of Hiroshima during World War II. Opponents said the play was "anti-American" and might give the idea that "America is unjust." [1]

While these two cases involved dramatic performances, other school controversies surround teaching methods and courses. Common targets are classes on AIDS, sex education, drug-abuse prevention, and programs designed to promote self-esteem or critical thinking.

In April 1992, the South Carolina state legislature considered a bill that would ban schools from using visualization, guided imagery, meditation, and relaxation techniques in classrooms.

Teachers have used these techniques to help students rest between difficult subjects, improve their memories, and use their imaginations. The bill's sponsor, Rep. Mike Fair, called these methods "religious New Age practices" meant to influence students' "subconscious minds." Fair also linked these practices to school violence and a decline in academic achievement.[2]

Textbooks are also often challenged. In Maryland, during the 1980s, a school board was asked to remove some second-grade reading texts. The National Organization for Women (NOW) said the books were "sexist," and showed women in old-fashioned roles.

Other texts and library books have been condemned for the opposite reason—because they show women who pursue careers instead of homemaking and child-rearing roles. Very conservative religious groups have opposed the nontraditional image. In 1991 alone, "Impressions," a series published by Holt, Rinehart, and Winston, was challenged forty-five times around America, for these and other reasons.

Textbook activists (often Christian Fundamentalists, who believe in a literal interpretation of the Bible), have pushed publishers to omit material they dislike or to include material that fits their values. Pressure comes from all sides, as people with liberal political views and those with conservative ones try to influence what goes into textbooks used all over America.

There have been numerous attacks on books used in schools. In 1976, a school board in Long Island, New York, decided to remove ten books from the Island Trees High School library. The board called the books "anti-American, anti-Christian, anti-Semitic, and just plain filthy."[3] Among the books were Eldridge Cleaver's *Soul On Ice*, Kurt Vonnegut's *Slaughterhouse-Five*, Bernard Malamud's *The Fixer*, Desmond Morris's *The Naked Ape*, and the *Best Short Stories of Negro Writers*, edited by acclaimed poet Langston Hughes. During the community debate, most students and parents protested

Pictured here are two of the students who brought charges against the Island Trees School District in Long Island, New York.

7

the removal of the books. They said their First Amendment right to receive information and ideas was being denied. The school board said it had a duty to "protect the values" of the community.[4]

The legal battle over these books went all the way to the United States Supreme Court, which decided *Island Trees School District* v. *Pico* in 1982. The Court said that the books should be returned to the library. Yet these issues are far from resolved to everyone's satisfaction. Since 1982, in thousands of other cases, books have been challenged or removed from public schools.

Besides attacking what students read, study, or watch, parents and others may try to limit what students may say or write. In Boynton, Oklahoma, an African-American student was urged not to recite Martin Luther King, Jr.'s 1963 "I Have A Dream" speech during a contest. High school officials said King's speech had "racial overtones" that might cause problems. Two dozen students boycotted the school for a week.

Officials have banned certain material from school newspapers. In 1983, at Hazelwood High School, near St. Louis, Missouri, journalism students wrote articles about teen pregnancy and the impact of divorce. The principal banned both articles. In its 1988 ruling, the United States Supreme Court sided with the principal.

These are examples of censorship in public schools, something that has increased steadily since 1980. Incidents occur in every state and touch all areas of education and school coursework. Every school has been affected in some way by censorship.

Censors may include local, state, and federal officials, teachers, members of the clergy, librarians, administrators,

Martin Luther King, Jr.'s famous "I Have A Dream" speech caused controversy when a student was not allowed to recite it for a contest.

parents, other citizens, and students themselves. As tax-supported institutions, public schools are seen as public property. Any member of the community may decide to ask teachers, librarians, or school administrators to censor books, materials, or activities.

Aside from individuals, about three hundred organizations of varying sizes in America are involved in censoring books in libraries or schools.[5] Some organizations join ongoing disputes; others begin them.

People who join such disputes often hold strong feelings and convictions about what people should read, write, learn, or see. Censors say they must protect students from materials that are upsetting or convey the "wrong" ideas—those that weaken parental authority; challenge their political, moral, or religious views; or "brainwash" students to other ways of thinking.

A different point of view says that freedom of expression helps to prepare students to function as adults. Those who oppose censorship say young people should be exposed to different ideas and the wide range of viewpoints in the real world. They believe censorship denies students the right to learn, think, and debate issues. This could limit their problem-solving and thinking skills.

Opponents of censorship also say that it interferes with academic freedom—the right of teachers to use methods and materials they find most effective. They claim it is unconstitutional—against the First Amendment—to limit what everyone can learn because certain ideas offend someone's political or moral beliefs.

Debates over censorship in schools are often bitter ones. People on both sides point out that young people are required to attend school during their growing years. Also, today schools are often faced with various social issues and problems, as well as educating young people for their adult lives and the modern workplace.

At the heart of these matters are questions of values and the meaning and purpose of education itself. The issues surrounding censorship in schools are complicated, with no clear-cut answers.

The following list shows the many targets of censors:

- Courses on drug-abuse prevention, sex education, character development, or values clarification; "situation ethics"—the idea that there is more than one right way to behave in a situation

- Assignments that ask students to share personal opinions and feelings; role-playing exercises

- Materials in history or social studies that show negative traits of famous historical figures

- Materials about other cultures labelled as "pagan;" multicultural studies (seen as "un-American")

- Works by authors considered to be "subversive" or "anti-war;" material about communism, socialism, internationalism

- Realistic novels for adolescents involving family conflicts, sex, drug use, teen pregnancy; books that criticize parents

- Books written by homosexual authors or those featuring likeable homosexual characters

- Materials dealing with harsh realities of life: war, crime, violence, sex, inner cities, racism, death

- Materials that discuss magic, the occult, the supernatural

11

- Materials that encourage understanding or acceptance of other religious traditions

- Books that feature cursing, sexual slang, or nudity

- Materials based on teaching values clarification, behavior modification, human development

- Sexist or racist statements or stereotypical characters

- "Role-reversal" in which women are shown as breadwinners, not in traditional homemaking or child-rearing roles

2

What Is Censorship?

A censor is defined as an official or government entity that removes or restricts books, plays, the news media, etc. in order to suppress information or ideas that are considered objectionable on moral, political, religious, military, or other grounds.[1] Censors say that they are trying to protect three basic social institutions: the family, the church, and the state.[2]

Author and English professor Lee Burress offers a broader definition, calling censorship "any effort to prevent the fulfillment of a communication."[3] This can be person-to-person contact or involve mass communication—the print media, radio, television, movies, recordings, and computer networks. Written communication (stories, plays, poems, or speeches) may appear in books, pamphlets, newspapers, or magazines. Visual forms include works of art and photographs.

Censorship occurs in various ways. One is through

laws that ban certain types of communication. In some countries, such laws cover a wide range of activities and affect many areas of life. Self-censorship occurs when agents of communication, such as writers, publishers, broadcasters, musicians, or filmmakers, follow codes or standards in producing their work. Communities or organizations may develop their own laws and guidelines. Social pressure in a community may also limit certain types of communication.

Censors focus on the ideas expressed in material rather than how well the material serves an educational purpose. They object for political or religious reasons. Often, they state objections in emotional terms, not as literary criticism.[4]

Censors may remove books or other materials from a library or classroom or limit access to them.[5] The materials are not illegal, but one or more people in the community disapproved of them. Says the National Coalition Against Censorship, a group of more than forty organizations that oppose censorship, "Activists place pressure on school boards by writing letters, making phone calls, attending school board meetings, circulating petitions, etc."[6]

Types of Censorship

Censorship may occur openly or so quietly that few realize it is happening. Some incidents become public. When challenges are public, other people know about them and can join the debate.

However, most censorship is done quietly by individuals, not groups protesting in public. Some call this "closet censorship." Individuals may send a formal complaint to school officials or quietly ask a librarian to remove a book. Librarians may avoid buying books if they fear people will object. Teachers may avoid using materials that have caused trouble in other schools. Curriculum committees may exclude books from reading lists and classroom use for the same reasons. Even those who believe in the value of a book or project may reject it, fearing parental complaints or lawsuits.

There is also censorship by theft. In Montello, Wisconsin, during the 1979–80 school year, a student checked out four books from the library, including three novels by Judy Blume. A best-selling author, Blume has been attacked for her realistic portrayal of children's feelings and life experiences. When the books were not returned, school authorities concluded that parents were purposely keeping them out of the library.

Many challenges are not reported. A school superintendent told author Edward Jenkinson that a woman had said her church would sue the school system if it bought a textbook that held two pictures of people playing cards. In her religion, card-playing is a sin. The superintendent told teachers to choose a different book.[7]

Censors and Their Targets

The American Library Association (ALA) has said, "Threats against the freedom to read come from many quarters, and many political persuasions are represented [by] those who would limit the freedom of others to choose what they read, see, or hear."[8] Most challenges come from conservative religious individuals or groups who believe in traditional roles for men and women and a strict interpretation of the Bible. Expressing this point of view is Janet Egan, director of Parents of Minnesota, Inc. She calls feminism:

> one of the greatest evils that has beset education . . . Women who are career-minded become less domestic-minded and can't take orders from a man. A career makes her unhappy, with less time for her husband and family. We can't all be bosses. Somebody has to be submissive.[9]

Groups like Egan's have worked to get their members elected to school boards. Board members can try to influence school policies to fit their values. Opponents of censorship are worried about the increasing number of conservative-minded people joining school boards. Arleen Arnsparger, a spokesperson for the Education Commission of the States, says, "It's happening everywhere. Entire communities are under attack, and it's only going to get worse. . . . They're saying that there needs to be a clear set of values in public education, and they just happen to be [their group's] values."[10]

A 1993–94 survey of 375 censorship attempts showed that they centered on sexual content, language, and religion. Thirty-one percent involved the treatment of sexuality, with strong objections to homosexual references and characters. In 26 percent of the cases, people objected to the language in a book. Examples here ranged from novels like *Of Mice and Men* and *The Catcher in the Rye* to *Merriam-Webster Collegiate Dictionary* and the Bible.

In 22 percent of the challenges, people claimed materials were "anti-Christian" or "endorsed a religion other than Christianity," such as "New Age" religion,

Satanism, or the occult. For instance, people objected to the words "shrine," "omen," and "seance" in Toshiko Uchida's story "The Best Bad Thing."[11] Says People For the American Way, a civil liberties group, "This tactic, defining new religions and finding them in everything from guidance programs to literary classics, presents an opportunity to remove any material that is not firmly grounded in the challengers' religious faith."[12]

About 6 percent of the challenges came from people with liberal political beliefs. They complained about materials that stereotyped or insulted women, African Americans, Native Americans, Jews, and others. Among the books they challenged were *Peter Pan*, the *Little House on the Prairie* series, *The Autobiography of Malcolm X*, and *Grimms' Fairy Tales*.[13]

Summarizing the potential targets of censorship, the National Council of Teachers of English (NCTE) has said:

> First, any work is potentially open to attack by someone, somewhere, sometime, for some reason; second, censorship is often arbitrary and irrational. For example, classics traditionally used in English classrooms have been accused of containing obscene, heretical, or subversive elements. What English teacher could anticipate judgments such as the following . . . Plato's *Republic*: "This book is un-Christian." Jules Verne's *Around the World in Eighty Days*: "Very unfavorable to Mormons." Nathaniel Hawthorne's *The Scarlet Letter*: "A filthy book."[14]

Often, people who wish to censor material have read only certain words or passages from it. The title may alarm them, as when parents tried to remove *Making It with*

17

The Reverend Jerry Falwell is the founder and president of the Moral Majority, a group that publishes lists of books to which it is opposed.

Mademoiselle from a school library. Closer examination showed that this book was a sewing guide by *Mademoiselle* magazine.

Some censors belong to large organizations that publish lists of materials they dislike. These groups offer guidance and legal help to individuals. These groups include: the American Family Association; Focus on the Family; California Educational Research Analysts, Inc.; the John Birch Society; the Ku Klux Klan; the Moral Majority; and National Legal Foundation. Two others, Concerned Women for America and Eagle Forum, opposed the Equal Rights Amendment and urge traditional roles for women. Citizens for Excellence in Education (CEE) is part of the National Association of Christian Educators. In 1992, CEE claimed it had 120,000 members in 868 chapters, located in every state. Membership was increasing by more than 100 percent a year.[15]

Increasing Incidence

Censorship attempts in schools have been increasing.[16] During the 1993–94 school year, the number of attempts had reached 462. About 42 percent of these known attempts succeeded in removing or restricting access to the materials in question.[17]

Censors have banned textbooks, magazines, library books, pictures, dictionaries, audiovisual materials, courses, programs, and homework assignments. Books have also been burned. In 1974, censors in Drake, North Dakota, burned *Slaughterhouse-Five* by Kurt Vonnegut to protest its language and political ideas; *Of Mice and Men* by John Steinbeck was burned in Oil City,

Pennsylvania, in 1977 by people who objected to the homosexual character. In 1981 in Omaha, Nebraska, censors burned many books, including *National Geographic* magazines (called "pornographic" because they contained photographs of women from cultures where breasts are not covered).

Professor Edward B. Jenkinson, former chairman of the National Council of Teachers of English (NCTE) Committee on Censorship, says, "censors have been successful in many instances because parents do not always take the time to read the books under attack, or to attend school board meetings, or to talk with teachers about their courses and course objectives."[18]

Censorship may not achieve the desired result. Some students seek out banned books. Also, in cases where people marked out words, students have substituted other, more extreme ones—for example, replacing "damn" with a worse four-letter word.

Censorship Versus Selection

People who try to prevent the purchase of certain books or other materials may claim they are helping schools to "select" the right materials. They point out that limited school and library budgets permit only a certain number of purchases.

Critics of this argument say that selection differs from censorship. Selection begins with the idea that all materials are potential purchases. While buying as many books as the budget allows, librarians choosing the books would not limit themselves to materials that fit their personal tastes and values. They might reject books that received negative reviews from respected educators or that duplicate materials already in the library, not because they wish to censor certain subjects or ideas. They seek materials for diverse needs, interests, and educational purposes.

Author Lester Asheim says that selection is democratic, while censorship is authoritarian. He writes:

> Selection's approach to the book is positive, seeking its values in the book as a book, and in the book as a whole. Censorship's approach is negative, seeking for vulnerable characteristics wherever they can be found—anywhere within the book, or even outside it. Selection seeks to protect the right of the reader to read; censorship seeks to protect—not the right—but the reader himself from the fancied effects of his reading. The selector has faith in the intelligence of the reader; the censor has faith only in his own.[19]

People For the American Way (PAW) says that in trying to identify a censorship attempt, we should ask two key questions:

"First, do the objectors demand removal of the material for all students, not just their own? Second, are objections ideological, sectarian, or otherwise noneducational in nature?" If the answer to both questions is yes, censorship is probably taking place.[20]

Who Decides?

Debates over freedom of expression in schools—over what is taught and how people express themselves—are among the most emotional, divisive issues in our nation. Critics of censorship argue that it limits the students'

21

right to read, learn, and be informed and also teachers' academic freedom.[21]

Others say they have a duty to set more limits. Parents of Minnesota, Inc., expressed feelings shared by others when it said:

> We charge that in the name of education, our children are taught Blasphemy, Profanity and Pagan religions, including Demon Worship. Our children's minds have been assaulted with grotesque and violent material, hopelessness and death. Educators have adulterated their students minds with alien philosophies under the guise of Academic Freedom.[22]

During a broadcast of the "Oprah Winfrey" show on October 10,1989, Robert Simonds, president of Citizens for Excellence in Education, said that censoring certain materials is a parent's right. Simonds complained that people who oppose his group seem "to think that parents don't have a right to question what their children are being taught. Their message to America's parents is simple: we know what your kids need to learn . . ."[23]

Donna Hulsizer, representing People For the American Way, countered, "That's not true. We welcome parents' involvement in the schools. But these are not parents who are simply concerned about what their children are reading. They want to make that decision for everybody else in the community."[24]

Another vocal critic of school materials is Phyllis Schlafly, an attorney, author, and founder of the conservative group Eagle Forum. Schlafly says that taxpayers should have a say about which library books are purchased. She calls this the public's "right of free

Phyllis Schlafly, shown here with Billy McCormack, argues that taxpayers have the right to give their input about which books are purchased for their local library.

speech and on how taxpayers' funds are spent and on what standards . . ."[25]

Using this reasoning, one could argue that African-American taxpayers need not pay taxes that are used to buy books that hold ideas that offend them. Women could refuse to pay for books that offend any women. But courts have rejected the idea that individuals can pick and choose what things the government can buy with their taxes.

As with any censorship, the issue of school censorship raises many questions: Who should decide? Teachers and other educators? School boards? Parents?

Individuals? To what extent can boards and administrators impose their moral, political, and/or religious beliefs on school materials and programs? What guidelines should people use in making these choices? How should schools respond when parents or others in the community ask that material be censored—not just for their own child but for all students?

Throughout history, governments have limited expression in various areas of life—cultural, political, religious, educational, and military. This was the rule, not the exception. Then, in the late 1700s, the founders of the United States envisioned a new kind of society, where freedom of expression was guaranteed by law.

3

Censorship Throughout History

Americans often say, "It's a free country—people can say whatever they want." While there are some legal limits on free expression, Americans have enjoyed such freedom more than any other nation in history. Early settlers embraced the idea of free speech and a free press, both restrained by the governments in their native lands.

Censorship in Earlier Times

Since ancient times, people in powerful positions have sought to control what information and ideas reached the public. Although ancient Greece adopted democratic principles during its Golden Age, censorship still took place. The famous philosopher Socrates (approximately 470–399 B.C.) chose to commit suicide rather than agree to censor his teachings. Ironically, his student Plato (approximately 428–347 B.C.) later supported the banning of art and literature that did not promote certain moral

Socrates was an early anticensorship advocate, choosing to die rather than censor his teachings. This is Jacques Louis David's painting *The Death of Socrates.*

principles. He also said that speaking against official views about religion should be a crime. During these years, books were burned. Greeks were persecuted for expressing unpopular ideas.

Around 213 B.C., Chinese Emperor Shih Huang Ti ordered that all past writings be destroyed. He told writers to start recording history anew, with his rule, as if the past had never happened. Much of ancient China's history and literature was lost, including works by the philosopher Confucius (approximately 551–479 B.C.).

In ancient Rome, free speech was a privilege reserved for emperors and other powerful people. Writers were banished for criticizing the government. Some books were burned. A writer who had offended Emperor Caligula was burned alive. The large, diverse Roman Empire included many religious groups. Roman leaders showed some tolerance but insisted that everyone pay homage to the emperor and his image. Christians and Jews who refused were persecuted.

Censorship by Religious Groups

After Christianity became the official religion in Rome in A.D. 313, the tide changed. Now those who criticized or rejected the Roman Catholic faith were persecuted. People were forbidden to speak against the pope, head of the church and a powerful political force. The papacy (office of the pope) issued a list of forbidden books in A.D. 496.

From 1231 to the early 1700s, the Church operated the Inquisition. The Inquisition investigated charges of heresy—speaking out against the teachings of the Church. Those who were found guilty might be fined, beaten, imprisoned, tortured, or killed.

27

The printing press became available in Europe in the mid-1400s. In 1487, church authorities required printers to seek permission before publishing anything—the beginning of pre-publication censorship. Works deemed anti-Catholic were condemned.

By the 1500s, protesters were leaving the Church to form new religions. Leaders of these new groups also often tried to censor their opponents. King Henry VIII established the Church of England with himself as leader, then persecuted Catholics and members of other Protestant groups. He burned versions of the Bible that he disliked and banned numerous other books.

Other rulers also banned books. In 1524, Charles V of Belgium issued a list of banned books, calling them a threat to the church. Censorship tended to be most sweeping in places where government and religious bodies were linked. Official religions limited what citizens could say, see, read, and discuss. In 1559, Paul IV published the *Index of Forbidden Books*, most of them about philosophy and religion. By 1948, the last year it was published, the *Index* included five thousand books.

Government Censorship

Under Henry VIII, all books had to be approved by royal officials before publication. Only licensed printers could produce books, and they were expected to control the content. Writers and printers were arrested for criticizing rulers or their actions. During the 1500s, under Henry's daughter, Elizabeth I, calling the queen a "tyrant, usurper, or heretic" could lead to imprisonment, the loss of a hand, torture, or execution.

A printing act passed in 1662 banned material that insulted the English government or Church of England. People could be put on trial for seditious libel (criticizing the government). In 1663, a printer was executed for printing a book that said rulers should be accountable to their subjects. The libel law remained in effect even after printing licensing laws were finally abolished in 1695.

By the 1700s, as newspapers and books grew in number, diverse opinions were being aired. Gradually, the English press became more free, too.

A Free Press Takes Root in America

Early Americans brought with them some traditional ways of limiting free expression. For example, in the colonies, it was a crime to commit blasphemy—curse or speak disrespectfully about religion or God. Newspapers had to be licensed by government officials, who were appointed by English rulers.

In 1721, Boston printer James Franklin was imprisoned for running a newspaper without a license and criticizing the English government. While Franklin was in jail, his brother Benjamin (later famous as an inventor, patriot, and diplomat) published the paper. Ben Franklin published part of an essay written in London, which said, "Whoever would overthrow the liberty of a nation must begin by subduing the freeness of speech."[1] This case, ending with Franklin's release, established a new legal principle: The government cannot censor something before it is published. This has become known as the ban against prior restraint.

A landmark case in the struggle for a free press took

29

place in the British Crown Colony of New York. Colonists resented the governor, William Cosby, who was considered both greedy and corrupt. During one scandal, Cosby removed a New York Supreme Court justice who had issued a ruling against him. John Peter Zenger, a former servant who became a printer, had been named publisher of *The New York Weekly Journal.* Zenger published articles criticizing Cosby's administration, as well as song lyrics that mocked Cosby.

Governor Cosby ordered that four "offending" issues of the *Journal* be publicly burned. On November 17, 1734, Zenger was arrested and charged with seditious libel, for "inflaming [the minds of the people] with Contempt of His Majesty's Government."[2] Zenger spent ten months in jail awaiting trial. Support for his cause swelled, and his wife and friends kept publishing the paper.

The Zenger trial was held on August 4, 1735. A prominent Philadelphia attorney, Andrew Hamilton, defended Zenger. Hamilton told the jury he would prove that the articles Zenger had published were true. The government argued that it made no difference whether they were true or false; maligning the government was a crime.

An eloquent Hamilton told the jury that citizens should have "the Right—the Liberty—of exposing and opposing arbitrary Power . . . by speaking and writing Truth."[3] To find Zenger guilty, he said, the jury must conclude that the words he had printed were "*false, scandalous, and seditious* . . ." He said that their decision would affect "the Cause of Liberty" itself.[4]

Within ten minutes, the jury had returned its

verdict: Not guilty. People inside the courtroom cheered, as did the crowds outside. After the Zenger case, the truth of a given statement became a legal defense against charges of libel in the colonies. People could disagree with the government or criticize public officials without fear of arrest.

The First Amendment

As the colonists demanded their independence from England in 1776, they developed a unique form of government—"of the people, by the people, and for the

This diorama of the Zenger trial is on display in Federal Hall in New York City, New York.

people." Later, America's leaders put their ideas about individual liberties in the Bill of Rights. These first ten amendments to the United States Constitution became law in 1792. Freedom of expression was seen as so important to a free society that it was written into the First Amendment, as follows:

> Congress shall make no law respecting an establishment of religion or prohibiting the free exercise thereof; or abridging the freedom of speech, or of the press; or of the right of the people peaceably to assemble, and to petition the government for a redress of grievances.

First Amendment rights encompass not only the right to speak freely but also include a much broader range of expression. The right to publish unpopular ideas and to "speak" symbolically, as by wearing a political button or carrying a banner, are protected.

James Madison, chief author of the Bill of Rights, staunchly supported free expression. He said this freedom could be threatened not just by tyrannical public officials but also when government has the power to act on behalf of a majority of citizens who want only *their* ideas to be heard.[5]

Limits on Free Expression in the United States

Despite the First Amendment, there have been laws limiting free expression. In 1798, under John Adams, the federal government passed the Sedition Act. The act allowed the president to punish those who criticized the government. Several newspaper editors were imprisoned

James Madison, author of the Bill of Rights, the first ten amendments to the United States Constitution, supported free expression.

for publishing critical articles. Thomas Jefferson, who opposed the act, had it repealed in 1800 during his presidency.

During the early 1800s, before slavery was finally abolished, southern states enforced laws against abolitionist (antislavery) literature or speeches. Several states had obscenity laws, like those in England, banning materials thought likely "to deprave and corrupt those whose minds are open to such immoral influences."[6]

The United States Supreme Court supported limits on speech in a 1919 case, *Schenck* v. *United States.* Justice Oliver Wendell Holmes said that, in some cases, "words are used in such circumstances and are of such a nature as to create a clear and present danger . . . It is a question of proximity and degree."[7] Using this "clear and present danger" test, speech that poses an immediate, clear threat to others can be illegal. One common example is that a person may not shout "Fire!" in a crowded theater when no fire has occurred.

Certain other types of behavior are also not protected by the First Amendment. In wartime, it is illegal to publish information about troop movements, which could threaten national security. Also forbidden are: false advertising; libel (written false, defamatory remarks); slander (spoken false, defamatory remarks); disturbing the peace; and giving out classified information.

Twentieth-Century Concerns

During the 1900s, courts have heard an increasing number of First Amendment cases. The Supreme Court has struck down state laws that abridged freedom of expression, saying that they violate the Equal Protection

34

President Thomas Jefferson repealed the Sedition Act, which allowed the president to punish those who criticized the government.

Clause of the Fourteenth Amendment. That amendment, ratified in 1868, is now viewed as guaranteeing citizens the protection of all ten amendments in the Bill of Rights, no matter which state they live in.

There was a lot of censorship in the world news during the 1930s. Adolf Hitler's Nazi party had seized power in Germany. Early on, they censored all institutions, suppressing other political and social ideologies. Nazi officials sponsored massive book burnings in 1933. In 1939, Nazi troops invaded countries throughout Europe and suppressed free expression there, too. Observing this process, the American Library Association (ALA) took a firm stand against censorship in its "Library Bill of Rights," published in 1939.

Freedom of political expression reached a low point

in America in the early 1950s. During these Cold War years, negative feelings toward the Communists governing the Soviet Union ran high. Senator Joseph McCarthy headed a Senate subcommittee investigating alleged communist activities. Many Americans, among them prominent government officials, writers, and scientists, were intimidated, accused of wrongdoing, and called to testify. McCarthy was later censured by the Senate for his tactics, with some calling McCarthyism a modern-day witch-hunt.

Religious Expression in Schools

American courts have done a difficult balancing act regarding religious expression in public schools. Government sponsorship of religion or a particular faith was banned by the first clause of the First Amendment ("Congress shall make no law respecting an establishment of religion . . ."). This principle is often called separation of church and state. The United States Supreme Court has held that school officials may not compose prayers for students, lead acts of worship, or force students to take part in religious acts.

Explaining these decisions, the Court has said that Americans come from hundreds of different religions. The Bill of Rights protects certain individual rights against the will of the majority. Even if most people in a school follow the same religion, they cannot impose their practices on others, just as politicians in the majority may not force their views on the minority.

How does the First Amendment protect religious speech in school? If students wish, they may pray in private or with a group if they do not disrupt school activities. They may read the Bible in their free time, choose religious books for book reports, discuss religious ideas, and study the role of religion in American and world history. They may meet after school on school grounds for religious clubs if their school permits other clubs to meet on school grounds. In these ways, religious speech—as opposed to school-sponsored worship—is protected like other speech.[8]

School Censorship: On the Rise

Although schools have been experiencing more conflicts over freedom of expression, censorship in schools and libraries is not new, either. Some American libraries banned *Tom Sawyer* and *Huckleberry Finn* soon after they were published (in 1876 and 1884), complaining about the "poor grammar." In 1911, public schools in Meriden, Connecticut, removed Shakespeare's *The Merchant of Venice* from the curriculum and libraries.

Besides removing or banning books, some schools "bowdlerize" them. A nineteenth-century man named Thomas Bowdler removed sexual references and other passages from Shakespeare's plays. He called his versions "family" Shakespeare. Deleting or covering up segments of a book became known as "bowdlerization." In the 1820s, Emma Willard, founder of the Troy Female Seminary in New York (the first institution of higher learning for American girls), was asked to paste heavy paper over certain pages in anatomy texts. Parents said pictures of human organ systems were "indelicate" for girls to see.[9]

In 1924, some people tried to prevent high schools

in Fresno County, California, from buying copies of the King James Bible for the library. The state supreme court said schools *could* buy the Bibles. It wrote, "The mere act of purchasing a book does not carry with it any implication of adoption of the theory or dogma contained therein, or any approval of the book itself, except as a work of literature fit to be included in a reference library."[10]

During World War I (1914–1917) and World War II (1939–1945), it was considered unpatriotic to use the German language. Many schools did not teach German. Nebraska even passed a law banning its teaching. The United States Supreme Court struck down that law in 1923, in the case of *Meyer* v. *Nebraska*. Nonetheless, Texas laws banned using the Spanish language in schools until recent decades.

Concerned about censorship in schools, the NCTE wrote *The Students' Right to Read* in 1962. It said, in part:

> The American public schools, for many years, have been faced with the problem of censorship. Many such problems have been fostered by groups who question the use of instructional materials that do not meet their moral, religious, political, cultural, or ethnic values.[11]

By the 1980s, censorship attempts had increased greatly. The ALA Office for Intellectual Freedom found that between 1979 and 1984, attempts in libraries rose from three hundred to more than one thousand a year. Most attacks on school books called them obscene. Yet, as of 1990, no book used in a public school had ever been found obscene by the United States Supreme Court.

Not only did censorship efforts rise after 1980, they became more aggressive. According to one analyst, censors are willing "to do far more than storm a few school board meetings to get satisfaction. They have picketed schools, pulled their children from classrooms, clogged [school administrators'] offices with [requests for information], campaigned to recall or replace school board members, blasted levies for bonds and tax increases, filed lawsuits, and attacked the quality of instruction."[12]

These activities in schools reflect today's social and political concerns. Many people are upset about high rates of crime and violence, drug and alcohol abuse, and pregnancy among unwed teens. They may blame these on the way schools are run, or on television, books, movies, and music to which young people are exposed.

Some Americans say the lack of religious observances in public schools has led to social problems. Many send their children to private religious schools. Paul A. Kienel, of the Western Association of Christian Schools, says that the Christian school movement has been growing rapidly. He explains, "The force behind it is that the Christian community is having trouble identifying with the public school system. Academically and morally, it no longer represents their views."[13]

School board meetings and many other school events are held publicly. Taxpayers may feel they own the schools and have the right to decide what is done there. Some parents are also troubled by changes in education. They may not understand what children are studying or why. Parents may dislike books that include topics that upset them or that they hesitate to discuss with their children.

The 1980 election of President Ronald Reagan brought a surge of political conservativism. With more political power, people who dislike new trends in education have become more vocal. Some protesters have organized themselves carefully to promote changes in schools. They may belong to national organizations that are trying to remove specific kinds of materials from schools.

Feminists and racial or ethnic groups who wish to see themselves portrayed in a certain way have become involved, too. In 1965, the Council on Interracial Books for Children (CIBC) was formed. One of its goals was to increase awareness of how white, middle-class people and values have long dominated children's books. The CIBC promotes literature reflecting the "aspirations of a multiracial, multicultural society."[14] It has objected to books, filmstrips, and other materials for "sexism, racism, materialism, elitism, individualism, conformism, escapism, and ageism."[15]

In *The Students' Right to Read*, the National Council of Teachers of English described the fight against censorship as "a continuing series of skirmishes, not a pitched battle leading to a final victory over censorship."[16]

By the 1990s, such incidents had occurred in every state.

Many have centered around school libraries as people wrestle with the question of what limits should be set on the reading materials available to students.

4

What May Students Read?
Battles over Books

A high school student in Arizona who planned to write a report on Mark Twain's *The Adventures of Huckleberry Finn* was told that the book was "not approved" for the school curriculum. He would fail the assignment if he used it. *Huckleberry Finn,* which some critics call Twain's finest work, is among the most commonly challenged books in America. It has been attacked both by people who say it contains racial slurs and stereotypes and by others who dislike the way white characters befriend and sympathize with black characters. Some schools have removed it from their library. [1]

Supporters of books like this one say such books can help students to understand America's past. They show the cruel effects of slavery, which also sheds light on the reasons behind the modern civil rights movement.[2]

In 1994, junior and senior high students in New Ipswich, New Hampshire, were studying E. M. Forster's

Mark Twain's book, *Huckleberry Finn*, is a highly controversial work. Above is the Mark Twain House in Hartford, Connecticut.

Maurice and May Sarton's *The Education of Harriet Hatfield*, when suddenly, the books were taken away. *The Drowning of Stephan Jones* by Bette Green was also removed. Those who attacked the books objected to their topic, homosexuality. The school board agreed they should be censored.[3]

One of the ten most often challenged books is J. D. Salinger's *The Catcher in the Rye*, published in 1951. In 1989, freshmen at Boron High School in Boron, California, were reading the book, when their teacher, Shelley Keller-Gage, was told to remove it from the classroom. Parents had complained to the principal about the "rough language." Yet the book was on the state-approved reading list. Keller-Gage said, "I chose this book because towards the end, there's a wonderful message of hope. For the kids, having a spokesman who goes through the low self-esteem, depression, and peer pressure that they themselves may be experiencing is important."[4] Teachers at Boron did not succeed in reinstating the book. However, they set up a procedure to handle future challenges.

Every week, someplace in America, controversial books are removed from libraries.[5] Some are literary classics—Steinbeck's *Of Mice and Men*, Pearl Buck's *The Good Earth*, Nathaniel Hawthorne's *The Scarlet Letter*, Stephen Crane's *The Red Badge of Courage*. More recently published books are also often challenged: Richard Wright's *Native Son*, Alice Childress's *Hero Ain't Nothin' But a Sandwich*, Maya Angelou's *I Know Why the Caged Bird Sings*, Alexander Solzhenitsyn's *One Day in the Life of Ivan Denisovich*, and Claude Brown's *Manchild in the Promised Land*. Contemporary young adult (YA) novels by such popular authors as Judy Blume, Norma Klein, Robert Cormier, S. E. Hinton, and Alvin Schwartz are also controversial.

Attacks from All Sides

Robert Cormier's 1977 novel, *I Am the Cheese* has been attacked many times and was censored in Massachusetts and Florida during the 1980s. Critics complain that Cormier's books are "anti-government" and might depress children. Cormier counters that there should be room in children's literature for books with unhappy endings: "Kids want their books to reflect reality, and they know that the good guys don't always win."[6]

A father himself, Cormier sympathizes with "the impulse to shelter children. . . ." But, he argues:

> Children start thinking on their own while they are still in the sandbox. Parents have to accept the fact that they are not always going to be the sun around which their children orbit. Once you acknowledge these things, you can grow with them, you can develop a real relationship with them. But if you try to control your children's fantasies, thoughts, and emotions, you'll just drive your children away from you.[7]

Some people attack books that highlight racism and the mistreatment of minorities, such as Harper Lee's *To Kill A Mockingbird*, in which a black man living in a small southern town is wrongly convicted of a crime. James Michener's *Hawaii*, Eldridge Cleaver's *Soul On Ice*, *The Diary of Anne Frank*, and Ken Kesey's *One Flew Over the Cuckoo's Nest* have been attacked for similar reasons. Critics say such books exaggerate problems in America's past and put authority figures or leaders in a bad light.[8]

Books for the very young are censored, too. During 1994 and 1995, Faith Ringgold's award-winning picture book *Tar Beach* was challenged in Spokane, Washington, and elsewhere. Critics said the book stereotypes African Americans as eating fried chicken and watermelon and drinking beer.[9] Ringgold based her book on childhood memories of picnics on the rooftop of her family's apartment in Harlem, New York, during the 1930s.

In Virginia, school officials removed the picture book *Families*, by Meredith Tax. It had been used in a family life course there for six years. Two parents complained that the book encourages lesbianism and glorifies divorce. In a letter to *The New York Times*, Tax wrote, "Are the parents of Fairfax County so deluded that they think the divorce rate is caused by children's literature? Are they willing to let a couple of hysterics determine their children's reading material? And is it too much to expect a school administration to stand up to this kind of nonsense, rather than to cave in without a struggle?"[10]

One of the most commonly challenged nonfiction books is *Go Ask Alice*, an anonymous account of a young girl's drug addiction. It was published by her parents after her death to warn other young people about drugs.[11]

Books mentioning sex are also frequent targets. Ninth-grade teachers in Erie County, Pennsylvania, used felt-tip markers to cover passages about the mating habits of apes in Dian Fossey's book *Gorillas in the Mist*. In 1976, in Anchorage, Alaska, People for Better Education objected to *The New American Heritage Dictionary*, calling certain words, including "ass," "tail," and "bed" offensive. The Anchorage school board analyzed the book and kept it. But the board in Cedar Lake, Indiana, called the dictionary obscene and barred it from classrooms.[12] In July 1994, the board of education in Okonee County, Georgia, voted to remove from school libraries all books containing "explicit sex and/or pornography." School officials said that the mandate was vague and might require them to remove thousands of books, including Shakespeare's plays and dictionaries. In response, the board cancelled the ban.

The National Organization for Women (NOW) objected to the way some words were defined. NOW said "macho" was not given enough negative connotations. NOW objected to definitions for

Books such as these, are banned for a wide variety of reasons.

"woman," "womanish," "machismo," and "macho." They also faulted dictionaries for omitting the word "chairperson" and for not including more biographical listings of women in the arts, science, literature, history, and politics. Pressure from NOW led Texas to remove five dictionaries from its list of approved textbooks.

These examples show that people may object to books for many reasons—the subject matter, specific scenes or language, the political or social views, even the "mood" of a story. In Alabama in 1987, the State Textbook Committee banned *The Diary of Anne Frank*, calling it "a real downer."[13] They banned Henrik Ibsen's 1879 play *A Doll's House* for its "feminist views."[14]

Some people want works banned because of the author's own lifestyle (for example, homosexuality) or politics (for example, Communist party ties). Author Lee Burress cites these kinds of attacks on: Henry David Thoreau, Ralph Waldo Emerson, Nathaniel Hawthorne, Herman Melville, Edgar Allan Poe, Willa Cather, Emily Dickinson, Edith Wharton, John Steinbeck, Sinclair Lewis, Ernest Hemingway, Hans Christian Anderson, Robert Frost, Tennessee Williams, William Carlos Williams, James Baldwin, and Edna St. Vincent Millay.[15]

Some censors also object to books that portray different cultures, lifestyles, or religions. In Loyal, Wisconsin, people wanted *Saturday Night Fever* out of the school library. They cited "four letter words" and said that "life in a poor Italian section of New York does not 'pertain to our style of life at all.'"[16]

Other people want *more* diversity in books and would like books to be free of sexism, racism, or anything perceived as derogatory toward certain groups.

However, this could mean censoring hundreds of books written in the past, including folk and fairy tales. Works by Longfellow, James Fenimore Cooper, Elizabeth Maddox Roberts, and Hemingway, are among those that might offend Native Americans or other groups. [17]

Along these lines, some Japanese Americans objected to books written by other Japanese Americans about their experiences in internment camps during World War II. Critics said these authors did not present the experience in negative enough terms. Author Lee Burress asks, "Should young people and our society generally be denied the opportunity to learn of the reaction that seems to have been held by at least some Japanese-Americans about their experience in the concentration camps? Who is to decide that?"[18]

Michael Farris, president of the Moral Majority for the state of Washington, says a double standard exists if librarians remove books people find racist or sexist but not those things that offend his principles. [19]

Addressing these concerns, the Iowa Civil Liberties Union (ICLU) has said, "Schools, of all places, should be the last to deal with bad ideas by sweeping them under the rug." Instead, said the ICLU, racism, sexism, and other ideas should be discussed openly.[20]

Complex Cases

Censorship battles may last for months and divide communities. In 1973, Bruce Severy assigned Kurt Vonnegut's *Slaughterhouse-Five* and James Dickey's *Deliverance* to his classes in Drake, North Dakota. After a student complained about the language in

Slaughterhouse-Five, both books were denounced at a school board meeting. Vonnegut's novel was called "a tool of the devil."[21] The board had copies of the book collected and burned. When Severy's teaching contract was not renewed, he sued the school board and won. The books were later declared permissible for eleventh- and twelfth-graders.[22]

During 1979–80, parents in Montello, Wisconsin, wanted to ban Sol Stein's book *The Magician* from classroom use. After reading excerpts of the book, some filed formal objections, saying it was obscene, trash, un-Christian, un-American, and critical of the American legal system.[23]

Newspaper editor Gene Conrad called the parents' objections irrational. To support his argument, he published racy excerpts from the Bible and said he would formally challenge it. Regional newspapers ran more than one hundred stories and letters on this dispute. A two-hour radio debate was held. The school's review committee recommended keeping *The Magician.* The debate continued, as the media followed the case and new school board elections were held.

Courts throughout America have heard cases about book censorship. In 1968, after *Slaughterhouse-Five* was banned in some Michigan schools, the state's court of appeals said:

> Vonnegut's literary dwellings on war, religion, death, Christ, God, government, politics, and any other subject should be as welcome in the public schools as those of Machiavelli, Chaucer, Shakespeare, Melville, Lenin, Joseph McCarthy, or Walt Disney. The students of Michigan are free to make of *Slaughterhouse-Five* what they will.[24]

Yet, in 1972, the United States Supreme Court declined to hear a case in which junior high school officials had decided to allow only parents to check out copies of Piri Thomas's *Down These Mean Streets*. Justice William O. Douglas disagreed with the majority, writing, "Are we sending children to school to be educated by the norms of the School Board or are we educating our youth to shed the prejudices of the past, to explore all forms of thought, and to find solutions to our world's problems?"[25]

In 1977, a poem triggered a major controversy in Chelsea, Massachusetts. "The City, to a Young Girl" appeared in *Male and Female Under 18*, a reading anthology. In the poem, a teenager describes how she feels when men on the street yell out sexual taunts. A parent criticized the poem's "street language," and the school board said the book must be removed from the high school library. Later, the board said the book could remain if the poem was cut out. A federal court judge disagreed, saying that school board members could not censor books to fit their own social or political tastes. Judge Tauro said, "What is at stake here is the right to read and be exposed to controversial thoughts and language—a valuable right subject to First Amendment protection."[26]

Joseph L. Tauro's decision is often cited as a vigorous defense of a student's right to read. He described libraries as places where students look for information and ideas, explore the unknown, and seek answers, while questioning and thinking. Tauro said, "The most effective antidote to the poison of mindless orthodoxy is ready access to a broad sweep of ideas and philosophies."[27] That same year, the Sixth Circuit Court of Appeals said that a school board in Ohio decided that Kurt Vonnegut's *Cat's Cradle* and Joseph Heller's *Catch-22* should remain in a library. The court called the library a "storehouse of knowledge" and declared that removing books from a school library posed "a serious burden upon the freedom of classroom discussion . . ."[28]

In Bay County, Florida, in 1987 the school superintendent banned sixty-four books including *Oedipus Rex*, *Hamlet*, and *The Great Gatsby*. He said the books contained profanity, vulgarity, and sexual situations that violated conventional morality. Teachers and forty-four parents filed a lawsuit saying that Superintendent Hall had banned books on the basis of religious beliefs. Hall said he had a duty to "restore Christian values to the schools of Bay County" and that one vulgar word in a book was reason enough to ban it.[29]

A frustrated parent wrote to the paper:

> It occurs to this writer that perhaps we are committing a grave error in teaching our children to read. If we eliminate reading skills, we can eliminate access to *all* English literature which may contain a lot of vulgar language. . . . Let us exercise full control over what our children learn by promoting full illiteracy in Bay County schools. . . . Illiteracy is our most effective weapon against books.[30]

Judge Roger Vinson heard the case in United States Eleventh District Court. He declared that school officials could not remove books just because they hold ideas with which they disagreed. But he said that school boards could regulate the content of libraries through policies and procedures designed for that purpose. The procedures could not be challenged but decisions about specific books or materials could.[31]

A dispute over censorship in school libraries finally reached the United States Supreme Court in 1982. A Long Island school board had removed nine books, calling them "obscene," "indecent," and "violent." After parents and students sued the school and lost, they appealed. In June 1982, the Supreme Court ruled in their favor, saying that the First Amendment does not permit public school officials to arbitrarily remove books from a library. Justice William Brennan said, "Local school boards may not remove books from school library shelves simply because they dislike the ideas contained in those books and seek by their removal to prescribe what shall be orthodox in politics, nationalism, religion, or other matters of opinion."[32]

That same year, citizens in Mead, Washington, debated whether sophomores should read *The Learning Tree*, Gordon Parks's semiautobiographical account of growing up in southeastern Kansas. A mother claimed that the book insulted Christianity and included "pornography." The school said her daughter could use a different book for the assignment and be excused during class discussions. The Moral Majority, a group that holds conservative religious and political views, filed a lawsuit on behalf of the student. They claimed that the book inhibited her religion and promoted a "godless religion" they called "secular humanism."[33]

The federal district court said the school had acted properly. Justice William Canby said that the book represented "a particular literary genre" and "simply informs and educates students on a particular social outlook forged in the crucible of black rural life."[34] Canby said the school was not endorsing Parks's views any more than those of other authors, among them John Bunyan or Dante, whose works they also assigned.[35]

Purpose of Libraries

In its *Freedom to Read* booklet (1952), the American Library Association said that libraries should strive to offer "the widest diversity of views" and be a marketplace of ideas for all citizens. It said, "Freedom is no freedom if it is accorded only to the accepted and the inoffensive."[36] Author Lee Burress agrees, and says "The librarian's own political views are irrelevant."[37]

Procedures for Handling Book Conflicts

Many schools have formal procedures to deal with challenges to books and other materials. Ken Donelson, a teacher at Arizona State University, suggests that schools develop these guidelines. They should begin by formulating a clear, honest statement of educational philosophy that makes it clear where they stand on *indoctrination* and *education*.[38] Donelson says:

> Education implies the right of students to explore ideas and issues without interference from anyone, parent or teacher or administrator. Indoctrination implies the right of those in charge of students to force onto students certain values determined by what purports to be the dominant culture. Deviations from the norm are possible in a system that proposes to educate. Not so in a system that proposes to indoctrinate.[39]

Donelson thinks each department should formulate a philosophy and rationale for planning courses and a written rationale for any long work that is used in class. He urges teachers to communicate with parents, explaining why and how certain materials are being used. Librarians can formulate a book selection policy. Each year the school board should reaffirm its support for the policy.[40]

People who complain should be treated tactfully, with respect. Donelson says, "Parents and citizens have a right to question our teaching materials or methods . . ." and stifling parents is "a dangerously temporary non-solution."[41] Schools should first require concerned people to meet with the teacher or librarian to discuss their concerns. Those who wish to pursue the matter should fill out a form. Putting their objections on paper forces people to make specific criticisms. Schools should have committees to mediate these disputes and make decisions after conducting a fair hearing.

No solution is likely to satisfy all people every time. But Donelson and others believe that a well thought-out procedure to handle challenges to the school curriculum will best protect the rights of all parties. They may prevent incidents from turning into bitter, emotional battles that divide communities.

5

Attacks on Teachers and Courses

Should teachers be allowed to discuss books that contain words or ideas that offend someone? Should they express personal opinions in response to student questions? Should schools conduct programs on drug-abuse prevention, sex education, family life, or character development? Should they be able to teach students about evolution, the Holocaust, or different cultures and religions? These questions have been debated all over America.

Who Should Choose?

Teachers have been fired for choosing certain materials. In 1970, an eleventh-grade English teacher in Alabama assigned Kurt Vonnegut's story "Welcome to the Monkey House." The principal called it "literary garbage" that encouraged free sex and the killing of old people.[1] The teacher tried to explain that the principal

55

had misunderstood its meaning. She was fired and sued to get back her job. The court ruled in favor of the teacher, agreeing that the principal had misinterpreted the story. It called the event "an unwarranted invasion of her First Amendment right to academic freedom."[2]

Sometimes, intimidation leads teachers to change lesson plans. A teacher in Texas stopped using *The Drowning of Stephan Jones*, a fictional book about the murder of a homosexual man, after being told she might lose her job.[3] It is possible that many teachers privately censor themselves for fear of attacks.

In cases where teachers are penalized for assigning material that someone considered offensive, courts examine the context of the situation—how the material was used and discussed in class. Judges have said that such incidents must be examined case by case.

Teacher Speech

In 1970, a federal court ruled that teachers are not permitted to gain converts for personal or political causes. The court said that teachers can be dismissed for using the classroom as a forum "to sway and influence the minds of young people without a full and proper explanation of both sides of the issue."[4]

A high school civics teacher was fired in 1972 after parents accused him of "propagandizing"—trying to impose his ideas on the students. During a discussion of race relations, in response to a student's question, the teacher had said he did not oppose mixed marriages. But the court found that the teacher had presented the issues fairly. It said teachers should not risk losing their jobs merely for discussing controversial issues in the classroom.[5] Courts have also ruled that teachers cannot be fired because of their politics. In 1969, Charles James, an eleventh-grade English teacher in New York State, protested against the Vietnam War. He also wore a black armband, an antiwar symbol and sign of mourning for those who had died. The principal forbade James to wear the armband at school. He said it was unethical to express such views in class and might cause student disruptions and a division among the faculty. When James refused, he was suspended, then fired.

James filed a lawsuit. For three years, his family, including four children, struggled economically as the case moved through the courts.[6] The federal district court ruled against James. An appeals court did not agree and said high school students are mature enough to be exposed to political debate: "It would be foolhardy to shield our children from political debate and issues until their first venture into the voting booth. Schools must play a central role in preparing their students to think and analyze . . ."[7] James later said, "if I hadn't fought on, I never would have felt free again."[8]

In 1970, an eighth-grade teacher in Connecticut let students lead the pledge of allegiance. She felt that she herself could not take part, as a matter of conscience. The teacher felt that the words "with liberty and justice for all" were not true for African Americans and others. After being fired, the teacher asked a federal court to decide her case. It ruled in her favor. Under the First Amendment, said the court, people may speak or not speak: "It does not matter that her expression took the form of silence."[9]

May teachers or school employees share their own books with students? In 1994, library aide Debbie Denzer loaned some of her books to seventh-graders who were working on a project about witchcraft in the Middle Ages. They had found nothing in the school library. One book contained excerpts from primary sources showing the oppression of women in history; the other was a critically acclaimed American Heritage survey of occultism in history.

Denzer knew of no rules that banned loaning students a book on the basis of its content. Yet after parents complained that the books were "feminist" and offended their religious beliefs, the principal urged the school board to dismiss Denzer, which it did.

Debbie Denzer was fired when parents complained that she loaned books about witchcraft in the Middle Ages to students for a school report.

Later, the county superintendent ordered that Denzer be reinstated, saying there was no basis under state law to fire her. The school board appealed, so Denzer sued in federal court. She said that her rights to due process of law—in this case, a fair hearing and clear basis for her dismissal—and the First Amendment rights of her students had been violated. The court agreed. Denzer was paid thirty-eight thousand dollars as compensation.[10]

Courses Under Fire

Faced with rising rates of teenage pregnancy, AIDS cases, drug abuse, and other problems, schools have implemented courses to address them. Such courses have been widely attacked.

During the 1992–93 school year, three of the top ten banned materials in schools were self-esteem related. These are often part of drug abuse-prevention programs, since research shows people with high self-esteem are less likely to abuse drugs. Schools that receive federal funding have been required to offer antidrug programs.[11]

Parents complained that "Pumsy in Pursuit of Excellence," one of the banned programs, taught humanism and Eastern religious practices. Students repeated phrases such as "I am me and I am enough."[12] The slogan meant that people do not need drugs. Critical parents found a psychiatrist who supported them and said that "suggesting reliance on an inner authority undermines the child's respect for external authorities like parents and teachers."[13] In a new version of "Pumsy," author Jill Anderson, a teacher, changed the phrase to "I am me and I am okay."[14] Children are not

59

asked to repeat the phrase, so critics cannot say they are "chanting." Anderson said the protests seemed "unfounded and reactionary."[15]

Conflicts over Writing Assignments

People have also objected when students discuss or write personal feelings and opinions. They have said that sharing feelings and opinions or discussing personal experiences is an invasion of privacy. In her book, *Child Abuse in the Classroom,* critic Phyllis Schlafly attacked schools that hold a philosophy "that rejects the idea of education as the acquisition of knowledge and skills and instead regards the fundamental task of education as therapy."[16]

In response to complaints, Senator Orrin Hatch sponsored the Protection of Pupil Rights Amendment, or Hatch Amendment, to the General Education Provisions Act. The amendment, signed into law in 1984, bans psychological or psychiatric treatment and testing in federally funded programs without express parental consent. People have used the amendment to challenge many aspects of the curricula. The guidance and counseling program was removed from an Oregon school after parents said it violated the Hatch Amendment.[17]

Educators say it is hard, and often unproductive, to avoid all subjects related to students' life experiences. They may ask that students take stands on issues, apply what they read to their own lives, or imagine how they would feel in situations like those in a story. Appeasing critics would make countless areas off-limits. How can teachers balance privacy concerns with educational needs? Edward Jenkinson suggests that they avoid questions about "delicate family matters" or secrets that might harm or embarrass students or their families. Teachers must be careful how they ask for information, leaving students free to decide what to share. If students volunteer personal information, it should be kept confidential unless it involves child abuse. Teachers are also advised to use journals carefully, tying them into the course content.[18]

Complaints About Sex Education

Parents have criticized sex education courses, especially when such courses discuss birth control, "safe sex," or homosexuality. Senator Jesse Helms tried to pass an amendment to an education bill that would deny federal funding to schools with programs "having the purpose or effect of encouraging or supporting homosexuality as a positive lifestyle."[19]

In 1994, Valley Central School Board in upstate New York banned the use of a filmstrip, *Families: Their Forms and Functions.* Some parents opposed a remark about homosexual couples in the teacher's manual and asked that Planned Parenthood, which mentions birth control and family planning, be taken off a list of community resources students might contact. Teachers and supportive parents presented their views and the film at a later school board meeting. The board found that objections were based on ideological grounds, so the film could not legally be kept from all students.

Some schools decide to remove these courses rather

than fight. Yet advocates of sex education point out that the teen pregnancy rate in America is the highest in any Western developed nation. Rates are lower in countries with sex education programs. According to Roz Udow, "Censorship promotes ignorance—not innocence . . . "[20]

New Areas of Conflict

By the 1990s, school officials said most objections to courses charged occultism, Satanism, New Age religion, or Eastern religion.

Teachers in one midwestern school were told to stop using deep-breathing exercises in health classes after Fundamentalist parents complained these were Eastern religion practices.[21]

Programs that aim to promote character have been criticized. Assistant superintendent and educator Dr. Henry Huffman developed a program around values he considered universal, including courage, loyalty, and respect for other people. A church-going Methodist, Huffman was surprised by intense opposition from religious groups.

At one school where the program was to be used, a parent asked a teacher, "Are you going to be teaching about homosexuals?" The teacher commented, "They're so afraid that in teaching respect and tolerance for others, we might respect and be tolerant of homosexuals."[22] Another parent expressed concern that teachers might use "psychological methods" to alter children's values. She asked whether the program was "An experiment with our children's system of moral development, their values, their character?"[23]

Decision Making and Academic Freedom

Who should decide matters like these? Conservative Christians in Vista, California, worked to get their candidates elected to the school board. Then they worked to ban drug-abuse education and self-esteem programs in the schools. They said the government should mandate prayer and Bible reading—using their version of the Christian Bible—in public schools. "It would be wonderful to see Scripture read in schools so that children learn the truth," commented Deidre Holliday, elected in 1990 to the Vista board. She said teachers should tell students that Christ is their savior.[24]

Teachers in Vista worked for an "academic freedom" clause in their contract. It permits them to teach "lawful material relevant to a course." One teacher said, "We feel beaten up and distrusted."[25]

What does academic freedom mean? Should it apply in colleges but less so in elementary and secondary schools? Some people say that teachers in younger grades have a captive, more impressionable audience and should not have full academic freedom. Professor Stephen R. Goldstein has said that we cannot conclude that the Constitution "allocates curricular decision making authority to the teacher . . ."[26]

Other legal scholars, and some courts, disagree. In Colorado, District Court Judge Richard P. Matsch struck down a school board's decision to ban ten books from classroom use. He wrote:

> To restrict the opportunity for involvement in an open forum for free exchange of ideas would not only foster an unacceptable elitism, it would also fail to complete the development of those not

63

going on to college, contrary to our constitutional commitment to equal opportunity. . . . Consequently, it would be inappropriate to conclude that academic freedom is required only in the colleges and universities.[27]

Evolution and Creation Science

A debate over teaching evolution has raged for more than fifty years. The idea of evolution—a scientific explanation of how complex life forms developed from earlier, simpler life forms—is not new. About twenty-five hundred years ago, Greek scholars suggested that some land animals were once sea animals that changed form in order to survive. Later, other scientists suggested that all life forms are linked and noted similar traits among various animals.

In the years that followed, scientists wondered why and how animals adapted or became extinct. In 1859, Charles Darwin published *On the Origin of Species.* Darwin had studied plant and animal species around the world and concluded that all present-day forms of life descended from earlier forms, dating back to a one-celled organism. Humans and apes, he said, descended from a common, apelike ancestor that lived millions of years ago.

Scientists debated Darwin's findings. Religious leaders joined the debate, since evolution contradicts ideas in the Old Testament, which states that the natural world was created by God during a period of six days, along with the first humans, Adam and Eve, and that all humans descended from them.

Scientists studied apes around the world and found

skeletons of earlier peoples, such as Neanderthals. They measured the age of the earth from layers in rocks.

As time went on, some mainstream religions accepted the new scientific findings and merged them into their faith, but some religious groups did not. Christians who held to a literal interpretation of the Bible became known as Fundamentalists. They believed that hearing about evolution might undermine their children's religious faith, so they worked for laws to ban it in various states. For example, texts mentioning evolution were removed from North Carolina schools.

> In 1925, Tennessee passed the Butler Act. The act made it unlawful for any teacher in any of the universities . . . all other public schools of the State which are supported in whole or in part by the public school funds of the State, to teach any theory that denies the story of the Divine Creation of man as taught in the Bible, and to teach instead that man has descended from a lower order of animals.[28]

The fines ranged from $100 to $500 at a time when teaching salaries were about $634 a year.

In 1925, John Scopes, a high school teacher in Dayton, Tennessee, violated the act by teaching evolution in science classes. During an historic trial, Scopes was defended by Clarence Darrow; William Jennings Bryan represented the state. The two men, both brilliant lawyers, held different views of religion and science. Bryan endorsed the biblical account of creation. He said that parents had "a right to say that no teacher paid by their money shall rob their children of faith in God and send them back to their homes skeptical infidels, or agnostics, or atheists!"[29]

65

At the opening of the Scopes trial in July 1925, antievolution books were being sold in Dayton, Tennessee.

Darrow countered that the Butler Act used the Bible as a "yardstick to measure every man's intelligence and to measure every man's learning."[30] He pointed out that great scientific strides had been made since the Bible was handed down. Darrow said interest groups should not have the right to dictate what schools could teach, based on their personal views. The Bible, he said, was a theological book that people had a right to read, study, and accept on the basis of their religious faith but should not be a guide for teaching science.[31]

Defense lawyer Dudley Field Malone, assistant attorney general under President Woodrow Wilson, added, "Science and religion embrace two separate and distinct fields of learning."[32]

In the end, as Scopes's lawyers had expected, he was convicted. Scopes said, "I will continue in the future, as I have in the past, to oppose this law in any way I can. Any other action would be in violation of my ideals of academic freedom, that is, to teach the truth as guaranteed in our Constitution, of personal and religious freedom."[33] Scopes and his lawyers had actually hoped he would lose so they could appeal to higher courts. But the state supreme court overturned his conviction on a technicality. That meant Scopes could not take his case to the United States Supreme Court.

In a case often called "Scopes II," Susan Epperson, a church-going high school biology teacher, challenged her state's antievolution law. *Epperson* v. *Arkansas* was decided by the United States Supreme Court in 1968. Justice Abe Fortas, who had followed the Scopes trial while growing up in Tennessee, wrote the opinion. It said that school boards cannot ban a scientific theory from being taught in public schools just because it conflicts with certain religious beliefs.[34]

The 1980s saw new efforts to limit evolution teaching. By 1981, twenty-three states had laws requiring a balanced treatment of evolution and creationism, the biblical account of creation. When Arkansas passed such a law in 1981, twenty-three people, including parents, teachers, and clergymen, opposed it. At the trial, scientists said creationism met no tests for a scientific theory. The court ruled the equal-time law unconstitutional.[35]

Dudley Field Malone, J. T. Scopes, and Clarence Darrow during the Scopes Trial in 1925.

Louisiana's equal-time law was also contested. When the case reached the United States Supreme Court, a brief signed by seventy-two Nobel prize–winning scientists declared, "creationism is not based on scientific research."[36] The Court struck down the Balanced Treatment for Creation-Science and Evolution-Science in Public School Instruction Act, saying that it aimed "to advance the religious viewpoint that a supernatural being created humankind."[37]

In 1989, the California Board of Education said that teachers should use only scientific fact, hypothesis, or

The Court that ruled in the *Aguillard* case, which struck down the equal-time law in 1987.

theory in science classes. The board said that divine creation, the purpose of humanity, and related subjects could be discussed in English and history classes or with students' families or clergy.

People who protest the teaching of evolution often say that it causes social problems. One protester wrote, "The more evolution theory is present[ed] and the less creation theory is presented, the less respect is given not only to Deity but society in general and to our students [*sic*] attitudes toward what is good and wholesome."[38]

Commenting on the issue, paleontologist Stephen Jay Gould said, "Science tries to understand and interpret the factual state of the world; religion deals with ethics and values."[39] Author Arthur Blake says, "We are free to believe what we want to believe, yet we must allow teachers the opportunity to acquaint us with the knowledge discovered by scholars, researchers, and scientists in every discipline."[40]

6

Textbooks on Trial

In 1990, Superintendent Jerry Stackhouse, of Willard, Ohio, faced a major controversy over elementary school textbooks. The school board had unanimously selected "Impressions," a reading series, for use in Willard. A group of forty to fifty parents said the books were "too morbid, violent, and negative" and promoted antifamily values. The parents demanded that their children be excused from classes where the books were used.[1]

When the school board refused to stop using the books, some parents sued, then organized to repeal the school's operating levy. Stackhouse received threats. One caller said that the superintendent, his wife, or one of their six children would "go" if the books did not. Stackhouse, who said he had never seen an attack so well-organized and aggressive, called the conflict "out and out war."[2]

Although censorship of textbooks has occurred in

In 1990, the "Impressions" reading series caused a great controversy for the residents of Willard, Ohio.

America since colonial days, the number of attacks has risen dramatically. These attacks are more aggressive, well organized, and better funded than ever. People who launch attacks often receive advice, legal help, and other resources from national organizations.

Attacks increased in the late 1970s, a time when more people noticed that textbooks had changed greatly since the 1950s. Stories in older readers featured married, two-parent families, usually middle-class, with one or two children. English professor Joan DelFattore, author of *What Johnny Shouldn't Read*, sums it up:

> Father wore suits and went out to work; mother wore aprons and baked cupcakes. Little girls sat demurely watching little boys climb trees. *Home* meant a single-family house in a middle-class suburban neighborhood. Color the lawn green. Color the people white. Family life in the textbook world was idyllic: parents did not quarrel, children did not disobey, and babies did not throw up on the dog.[3]

Textbooks reflected changing times and concerns. During the 1960s, movements for civil rights and women's liberation took hold. People showed more concern about poverty, pollution, avoiding a nuclear war, and other social problems. Publishers showed lifestyles besides those of white, middle-class people in nuclear families. Among the new educational themes were multiculturalism—the study of different cultures and their impact on civilization—and environmentalism—the impact of industrialization and human activities on the earth and its natural resources. Books opposed racism and the stereotyping of women and minorities. They showed history as experienced by Native Americans,

73

African Americans, and other groups, not just white European settlers.[4]

Parents who disliked the changes began to protest. In 1986, a highly publicized conflict over a series of reading books took place in Church Hills, Tennessee. Leading the opposition were parents who formed Citizens Organized for Better Schools (COBS). They called the books "anti-God, anti-American, and anti-family."[5] One passage COBS disliked showed a girl (Pat) and boy (Jim) preparing raisin pudding and other food. It began: "Pat has a big book. Pat reads the big book. Jim reads the big book. Pat reads to Jim. Jim cooks."[6] Robert B. Mozert attacked the idea that Jim cooked before Pat did. He said this kind of story may give children the notion "that there are no God-given roles for the different sexes."[7] COBS also protested symbols in the book, claiming that nonverbal communication is a part of New-Age religion. Parts of the book were said to promote "secular humanism," a philosophy that emphasizes humans rather than God.

When COBS sued the school, the trial court ruled in their favor. The federal appeals court disagreed, saying that the Constitution does not require schools to substantially change their curricula in order to accommodate some students' religious beliefs.[8] Other critics say the lowest level of education will result if individuals and groups can force everyone to study only those materials or ideas that offend nobody.

States have tried to accommodate students' beliefs. Students can sit in another room or read alternate texts and books. But school officials find it impractical to excuse a student each time a controversial subject or

In recent years, textbooks have been including more multicultural history. Current history texts, for example, include Native American leaders, such as Chief Joseph of the Nez Perce tribe.

activity arises. Some excused students may feel uncomfortable. Other students may use the controversy as an excuse to avoid attending class.

Prepublication Censorship of Textbooks

Previous chapters have shown how censorship occurs before a work is published. During the 1970s, observant students informed author Ray Bradbury that a reference to abortion was missing from a textbook version of his anticensorship novel, *Fahrenheit 451*. Bradbury said that editors who were "fearful of contaminating the young, had, bit by bit, censored some 75 separate sections from the novel."[9] He notes that in the plot of his novel, books were first burned by minorities, "each ripping a page or a paragraph from this book, then that, until the day came when the books were empty and the minds shut and the libraries closed forever."[10]

Textbooks are designed for mass markets, since publishers cannot afford to produce different versions of the same book for different markets. Twenty-two states* currently require that schools buy only textbooks that have been approved by state committees, so their decisions can greatly affect sales. The two largest markets are Texas and California. In both states, especially Texas, activists have controlled much of what went into—and stayed out of—books.

*Alabama, Arizona, California, Florida, Georgia, Hawaii, Idaho, Indiana, Kentucky, Louisiana, Mississippi, Nevada, New Mexico, North Carolina, Oklahoma, Oregon, South Carolina, Tennessee, Texas, Utah, Virginia, and West Virginia

According to Bill Honig, a prominent educator who served as California's Superintendent of Public Instruction:

> Textbook publishing is a commercial enterprise and books are written for the nation, not a district. They respond to the market-place. It's understandable that, if someone is going to object, and they'll lose a sale because of it, they will write the books differently. They will keep diluting everything to avoid objections if they think that will make it easier for them to sell books.[11]

Early in the production process, publishers usually submit a book to the Texas and California boards for review. These boards can accept it, reject it, or ask for changes. Both states have curriculum guidelines and require publishers to show, with charts, how their books fit these guidelines. Although these states have different programs, publishers must cover the topics required by both states. Critics say this results in a superficial look at too many topics, with little in-depth coverage or absorbing writing.

Individuals and groups receive copies of the books and submit their opinions and recommendations. Two of the best-known textbook activists are Texans, Norma and Mel Gabler. The Gablers, neither of whom is a teacher or college graduate, founded Educational Research Analysts in 1961. The couple was upset about their son's schoolbooks—for instance, they thought his history book emphasized federal authority and neglected states' rights.

Since then, their organization has analyzed materials, searching for any items listed on a three-page handout written by the Gablers. Their concerns include passages they find unpatriotic, anticreationist, anti-traditional family, anticapitalist, too feminist, humanistic, communistic, or socialistic.

During the textbook-adoption process, examiners suggest changes. These changes may be extensive, as shown in a ninety-page protest against certain literature, written by a representative of the Texas Society of Daughters of the American Revolution. Among her suggestions: Delete Shakespeare's play, *Romeo and Juliet*, lest it promote teen suicide. Omit poems by African Americans dealing with racism, because they were "Communist propaganda" that reflected dishonor on the United States. Avoid works by Edgar Allan Poe since he was a cocaine addict. Delete *The Diary of Anne Frank* (too sad). They could be replaced by works by authors like Booth Tarkington and Eleanor H. Porter (who wrote *Pollyanna*). The same critic viewed literature anthologies produced for high schools as part of a leftist movement to sabotage the nation.[12]

Another critic declared in 1985 that the writing of various African-American poets and playwrights be omitted because of their political beliefs. She also asked the Texas board to remove some material on racism in history—Jim Crow laws, lynchings, denials of voting rights, segregation—saying these things would give students "a bad impression of the United States and foster racial hatred."[13]

Perhaps less than half of the suggestions made by critics in Texas are rejected. These include requests that publishers deny well-accepted facts, such as when someone objected to a text saying that the Church of England broke from the Roman Catholic Church.

As discussed in the previous chapter, textbook coverage of evolution versus creationism is highly controversial. For decades, textbook publishers omitted evolution or mentioned it only briefly. Attempts at compromise have not been satisfactory to either side. Creationists complain when books imply evolution is a fact; scientists complain that books do not cover evolution well and do not show that it is the unifying theory of biology.

By 1989, Texas was ready to consider a new measure that required high school biology texts to include a section on evolution. At the hearing, antievolutionist Daniel H. Harris told the board that creationism also should be taught if they planned to teach about evolution. Other opponents claimed evolution is linked to Nazism and communism and may lead to "suicide, cults, drugs and abortions of teenage pregnancies."[14] Some creationists argued that evolution gives the impression that humans are animals and thus removes moral and social restraints on behavior. One man said that this idea supports "the sexual revolution, because animals may copulate freely without the condemnation of God or men."[15] Antievolutionists also point out that some scientists, including Michael Denton, author of *Evolution: A Theory in Crisis*, have challenged the theory of general evolution on scientific not religious terms.

Against strong opposition, the Texas board decided textbooks must include a section on evolution. The measure said that schools could teach other "reliable" theories as well, along with evidence contrary to evolution.[16] In 1990, the board went further, asking publishers to expand coverage of evolution and to state that:

> There are virtually no differences of opinion among biologists, and indeed nearly all scientists agree on the following major points regarding evolution: (1) the earth is about 4.5 billion years old. . . . (2) organisms have inhabited the earth for the greater part of that time and (3) all living things, including human beings, have evolved from earlier, simpler living things.[17]

Supporters of the measure said it would finally let textbook publishers differentiate between science and religion. Yet the debate is far from over. In some places, people who do not like material about evolution rip pages from textbooks.[18]

Impact on Textbooks

Many critics say that these controversies over textbooks have led to "dumbed-down" books that lack depth and fail to address some important issues. Afraid of controversy, publishers have avoided or skimmed such subjects as sex, birth control, and political activities that show America in a negative light. One of their deepest influences, says author Joan DelFattore, is "to present religious figures and events in a wholly favorable light by twentieth-century standards, divorcing them entirely from violence—regardless of the facts."[19]

In one instance, the Gablers asked that the New Deal, political reforms implemented by the Roosevelt administration to ease the Great Depression, be omitted from a timeline of important events in United States history. They consider New Deal legislation to be socialism, something they deplore. The book's publishers explained that including something was not an endorsement but merely acknowledged the event's importance in history. When the Texas board refused to accept it, the publisher agreed to leave out that entry.

Censorship efforts also increase the cost of textbooks. More people spend more time reading complaints and suggestions and revising the books. DelFattore writes about the educational impact:

> When students have spent twelve years reading books based more on market forces than on scholarly excellence, they may not come to college prepared to do college-level work. [According to a report by the American Association of University Professors (AAUP)] students whose pre-college education was based primarily on "official" textbooks are not likely to understand how to deal with shades of meaning or with controversial topics.[20]

Analysts have concluded that the Texas board has resisted attempts to exclude minorities from textbooks and did, in fact, ask for more portrayals of not only African Americans but also Asians and Hispanics. In California, a 1976 textbook content law requires more coverage of women and minorities and their role in history. The Texas board has sought changes that show women in various roles and use the word "human" instead of "man" when both genders are being discussed.

The debate over textbooks shows no signs of ending. Controversy also surrounds another area of expression in the schools: what students may say (or not say), write, and wear.

7

Student Expression

In 1974, Priscilla Marco, a senior at a New York high school, wrote an article for the school paper. She told students that they had never been given copies of a New York City board of education pamphlet listing their rights and responsibilities. Marco also described incidents in which the principal had censored material from the school paper, *Skyline*, despite a board of education statement that the judgment in student newspapers should reflect their editors' decisions. The principal said Marco's article could not appear in the paper. He called it "irresponsible and badly written."[1]

Marco contacted the ACLU and school authorities. When the New York City school chancellor ordered that her article appear in the *Skyline*, the principal ignored it. However, on June 23, 1975, members of the board of education, along with security guards, entered the school. They passed out copies of a special edition of the

Skyline they had had printed. It discussed First Amendment freedoms and their meaning in the education of young people. Former New York City school chancellor Harvey Scribner said, "A student press should provide for opinions that differ, including faculty opinions. This is the place where distortions or misstatements are brought out for all to see."[2]

This is one of many cases dealing with the issue of how students may or may not express themselves. For decades, schools and the courts have worked to balance the rights of students to express themselves and the needs of schools.

The Student Press

Who decides what students may write in the school paper? In 1973, at Alabama's Troy State College, student Gary Dickey wrote an editorial in the *Tropolitan,* the college's weekly paper. It criticized the state legislature for its treatment of the president of the University of Alabama. The president of Troy State forbade Dickey to publish the piece. He said the editor of a paper should not criticize the owner (in this case, government officials or the board of trustees). In protest, Dickey ran an article that showed only his title, followed by a large blank space with a slash across it marked "ccnsored." A Montgomery newspaper printed it, along with a story about the incident.

That summer, Dickey was notified he would not be readmitted to the school. By Alabama law, a student refused admission to one school could not attend another. With help from the ACLU, Dickey sued to be readmitted.

He claimed that he was denied due process of law and his right to free speech. The college responded that their rules were needed to maintain order and discipline.

Ruling for Dickey, Judge Frank M. Johnson, Jr., said:

> A state cannot force a college student to forfeit his constitutionally protected right of freedom of expression as a condition for his attending a state-supported institution. . . . Teachers and students must always remain free to inquire, to study and to evaluate, to gain new maturity and understanding.[3]

The college was ordered to readmit Dickey and to pay all court costs.

A survey taken in the late 1960s showed that about 85 percent of all college newspapers and a larger number of high school papers were censored to some extent.[4] During the mid-1970s, another survey concluded, "Censorship and the systematic lack of freedom to engage in open, responsible journalism characterize high school [newspapers]."[5] Many students are used to accepting the decisions of school officials, without question.

One New Jersey student, Brian Desilets, *did* question school officials who banned reviews of *Mississippi Burning* and *Rain Man*, two R-rated movies, which he had written for the school paper. He won his case in 1994. The state Supreme Court said it could find no "legitimate pedagogical [educational] concern" to justify the school's action. The Court did say, however, that a school *could* develop such a policy, in writing, along with a clear rationale.[6]

School administrators say censorship is sometimes

needed to avoid disruption. The Student Press Law Center in Washington, D.C., says that, to justify censorship, administrators need "concrete facts that disruption will occur" so that disagreement with student views is not their main standard. The center says, "The fact that the views expressed may be highly controversial, critical of school officials, unpopular or in poor taste are never grounds to restrict student expression."[7]

In 1988 in *Hazelwood* v. *St. Louis Independent School District*, the United States Supreme Court said that student journalists do not have the same free speech rights as adults, so school officials may censor school newspapers to some degree. Three journalism students at Hazelwood East High School near St. Louis, Missouri, had written an article for their paper, the *Spectrum*, in which they described the experiences of pregnant students, without using their names. Another article discussed the impact of divorce on young people. The principal deleted both articles, calling them "inappropriate and unsuitable."[8]

The students sued on the basis of freedom of speech and press, but a federal judge ruled in favor of the school. Then a court of appeals ruled for the students, saying that the newspaper was a public forum, run for students as a vehicle for their opinions. However, the United States Supreme Court supported the school. Justice Byron White said that although students do not "shed their constitutional rights at the schoolhouse gate," they do not automatically have the same rights as adults outside of schools. A school is a special setting with "special characteristics," said White. Officials of a school need not permit speech that is "inconsistent with its basic educational mission." White also said the paper was *not* a public forum, since the general public was not allowed to use it as a medium to express their ideas. He said the school saw the paper as part of the educational process, subject to control of the school staff. Besides sponsoring the paper, the school gave students a grade for their work, and a teacher edited the paper. White said that schools have a right to exercise "control over the style and content of student speech in school-sponsored expressive activities."[9]

In a dissent joined by Justices Marshall and Blackmun, Justice Brennan said, "The young men and women of Hazelton [*sic*] expected a civics lesson but not the one the court teaches them today."[10] These justices said that school speech deserved protection similar to that of other speech. Following this decision, critics worried that school officials would have broad powers to censor students' viewpoints on a variety of grounds. Calls to the Student Press Law Center in Washington, D.C., rose from 548 in 1988 to 1,402 in 1994. Students and newspaper staff advisors increasingly sought legal assistance.

Student-Produced Papers

What about student-written papers produced outside the school? In 1971, Charlie Quartermain was suspended for passing out copies of a newspaper he had written off school grounds. His North Carolina high school had a rule that prohibited students from "distributing, while under school jurisdiction, any advertisements, pamphlets, printed material, written material . . . without the express permission of the school."[11]

In court, Quartermain said that his First Amendment rights to free speech and a free press had been violated. He lost in the district court, but the court of appeals found the school rule unconstitutional. The judges said there must be specific rules telling what students were banned from distributing. The court also suggested setting up a review board so that students could appeal any bans set by the principal alone. They noted that the rights of students, especially younger ones, were more limited than those of adult citizens.[12]

In 1972, some Chicago high school students passed out copies of a newspaper they had created on their own. They were suspended for violating a rule banning the distribution of literature on school premises, unless the superintendent of schools first approved it. A court of appeals ruled the suspensions were unjust. The court said that distributing the paper had not upset school discipline. The court forbade the board of education from censoring it through prior restraint—censoring something before publication.

In 1978, John Tiederman and three other students started *Hard Times,* a publication that mocked students and teachers. The group edited the paper after school in one of the teacher's offices. That teacher pointed out grammatical errors and suggested omitting certain articles. He advised the students to distribute the paper off school property and tell people that it was not school-approved. The students sold *Hard Times* at a grocery store. After seeing a copy, the president of the board of education urged the principal to punish the authors. The principal was upset that the paper had been typed and stored at the school.

There were no school publications, so the school had no rules to apply. But a state law said that students could be suspended for being "insubordinate or disorderly" or for conduct that "endangers the safety, morals, health or welfare of others."[13]

The suspended students sued, claiming that their free speech rights had been limited. The court of appeals agreed with the students, saying that the paper had been "conceived, executed, and distributed outside the school."[14] The United States Supreme Court refused to hear the case, so the ruling stood.

While the Tiederman case showed that off-campus papers might be permissible, it did not say that *any* type of paper could be produced on school property. Also, the United States Supreme Court has never said that prior restraint can never be applied to student newspapers. Lower courts have ruled that when a school administration sets clear guidelines about what a paper may or may not publish, they can enforce those guidelines. Such guidelines usually involve obscene or libelous language.[15]

Verbal Student Expression

Courts have ruled that schools may censor certain kinds of speech. In 1984, a high school senior was suspended for making a sexually suggestive speech, with innuendos rather than graphic words, during a school election campaign. The United States Supreme Court said, "The First Amendment does not prevent the school officials from determining that to permit vulgar and lewd speech such as [the plaintiff's] would undermine the school's basic educational mission."[16]

Hate Speech

In recent years, society has debated what to do about a category of expression known as "hate speech." Some high schools, colleges, and universities have codes that forbid spoken or written attacks on others based on race, gender, national origin, religion, color, sexual orientation, or handicap. In some cases, college students at both private and public schools have been expelled for using racial slurs or other language banned by the codes.

In 1990, a federal district court declared unconstitutional a hate speech code at the University of Wisconsin. The university banned racial, religious, and sexual slurs, because it believed these can create a "hostile learning environment."[17]

Should hate speech receive First Amendment protection? Those who say no point out that it is important to eliminate racism and sexual harassment from society. They say hate speech in schools can lead to violence and interfere with equal educational opportunity.

Those who oppose banning hate speech say that when these rules are too broad, officials can censor opinions or other speech. They point to cases like one at the University of California–Los Angeles where students were suspended for making satirical and critical remarks about affirmative action. Some critics say speech codes go to extremes, banning what amounts to bad manners. As an example, author Anthony Lewis cites a University of Connecticut rule that "prohibits inappropriate laughter."[18] He writes, "More and more of us seem to find our sensibilities so offended by someone's words that we rush to the law to demand punishment of the speaker. . . . Whatever happened to the American idea of freedom for unpleasant speech? And to our sense of the absurd?" Lewis is among those who say the best way to deal with bad speech is to answer it.[19]

In 1994, Howard University president Franklin G. Jenifer was criticized for not censoring speakers on campus who made anti-Semitic statements. Jenifer wrote:

> Some have asked me why I didn't simply ban Mr. [Khalid Abdul] Muhammad and others espousing similar views. That might have been the easier course, but would it have been the wiser one? As a deep believer in First Amendment rights and academic freedom, I have taken the position—all too often unpopular—that speech should never be suppressed unless it directly endangers lives. It is far better to allow the expression of hateful views in the light of day, where they can be exposed for what they are: vile, hurtful, insensitive—and wrong.[20]

Some college students who disliked what was published in their newspapers have turned to violence. At Brandeis University, the paper carried a paid advertisement from a Holocaust revisionist history group—people who say the Holocaust never happened or that the deaths and suffering have been exaggerated. A group of students later trashed the newspaper office.

Floyd Abrams, a First Amendment lawyer, says that destroying newspapers because one disagrees with the content is "antithetical to First Amendment values."[21] Abrams advises newspapers to publish advertisements or articles they find offensive but to include editorials that denounce the hateful ideas.[22] However, Professor

Catharine MacKinnon, an author who supports laws to curb pornography, says newspapers should not publish ideas they think are false or "lies that target groups of people for abuse and aggression in that community."[23] She does not support the particulars of every hate speech code but thinks some codes do protect people's right to equal access to the benefits of education.[24]

Deciding where to draw the line—between speech that makes people feel bad or hurts their feelings and speech that poses a danger or threat to education—will likely remain controversial.

The Right *Not* to Speak

Since its inception, the First Amendment has been interpreted as allowing people freedom *from* expression, too. A famous 1943 First Amendment case involved schoolchildren in West Virginia who refused, because of their religious beliefs, to take part in the morning flag salute, as required by state law. Here, both freedom of expression and religious freedom were at issue.

The United States Supreme Court ruled that students could not be legally required to recite the Pledge and could remain silent during that time. In a famous opinion, Justice Robert H. Jackson spoke about the rights of individuals to hold their own opinions and beliefs without being forced to accept the ideas of others. Throughout history, Jackson commented, those who tried to force a unanimity of opinion often ended up exterminating dissenters, leading to "the unanimity of the graveyard."[25]

Other students have refused to recite the Pledge for political reasons. In 1969, Mary Frain, a high school student in Queens, New York, did not believe there was "liberty and justice for all" in America. School rules required that those who refused to join the Pledge leave the room, but Frain refused, since this was widely viewed as a punishment. A Federal District Court agreed that Frain should be allowed to remain in her seat during the Pledge.[26] In a 1977 case in New Jersey, Deborah Lipp, who also objected to words in the Pledge, was told she must stand at attention during its recitation, but was not required to repeat the words or salute. When Lipp challenged this New Jersey law, she was ridiculed and received threats and abusive mail. Her parents also disapproved.

However, Lipp said that she had the duty to follow her conscience. She also asserted that she *was* patriotic and deeply appreciated the Bill of Rights as well as living in a nation where she could fight a law she did not like.[27] A federal judge overturned the law that required students to stand. He said that it forced people to affirm beliefs and express an idea contrary to their own.

Nonverbal Expression

Verbal expression is more often at issue, but some major school censorship cases involve symbolic—nonverbal—speech. A 1965 case, *Blackwell* v. *Issaquena County Board of Education*, began when students wore freedom buttons to school to support a voter registration drive. The school banned the buttons after students began pinning them to each other and throwing them, disrupting class. The court agreed with the school. It said there are limits to free speech, and each case must be decided on own merits.[28]

The United States Supreme Court has said that while silent communication about one's views is acceptable, schools can forbid disruptive acts, such as making speeches or carrying banners around the classroom. Courts have agreed that people may not air their views or protest any time, in any place, or however they please.[29]

In 1968, the United States Supreme Court heard the case of three teenagers who had engaged in symbolic political protest in Des Moines, Iowa. Mary Beth Tinker, her brother John, and Christopher Eckhardt were suspended for wearing black armbands to protest the Vietnam War. They were told not to wear the armbands at school. The issue was hotly debated in the media and at school board meetings. The Tinker family received hostile phone calls and some death threats.

The young people, supported by their parents and the ACLU, sued. At the trial, they claimed a First Amendment right to peacefully express their views and dissent by wearing these symbols, as long as these were nondisruptive. Administrators asserted a right to make rules that protect the functions of the school and the well-being of students. One principal said, "The schools are no place for demonstrations."[30]

The trial court said that the armbands were not a form of speech that should be covered by the First Amendment. The court noted that people held strong feelings about the war and there might be school disruptions. The appeals court ruled against the students, too. It said that even if armbands were a form of protected speech, students could wear them elsewhere.

The United States Supreme Court decided *Tinker* v. *Des Moines* in 1968. Writing for the Court, Justice Abe

Mary Beth Tinker, seated next to her mother, was suspended for
wearing a black armband to school in protest of the Vietnam War. A
court battle ensued.

Fortas declared that wearing a symbol—in this case, a black armband—*was* a form of speech protected by the First Amendment. He said the school could not deny students this right unless a compelling interest was at stake. A "compelling interest," said Fortas, meant more than a "vague fear of disturbance," or the desire to avoid discomfort, or an unpleasant atmosphere; the form of expression must be such that it "materially disrupts classwork or involves substantial disorder or invasion of the rights of others." The Court found that armbands did not pose a "clear and present danger" anymore than religious symbols or political buttons, both of which were permitted in the school. If other students became unruly, said the Court, the school should discipline them rather than limiting free speech rights. In words that have been quoted often, Fortas said, "It can hardly be argued that either students or teachers shed their constitutional rights to freedom of speech or expression at the schoolhouse gate."[31] The Tinker case was called a landmark decision because it defined the free speech rights of students more clearly than ever.

In a dissent with Justice John Harlan, Justice Hugo Black said, "I disclaim that the federal Constitution compels teachers, parents, and elected school officials to surrender control of the American public school system to public school students."[32] Black, usually firmly on the side of free expression, said, "I have never believed that any person has a right to give speeches or engage in demonstrations where he pleases and when he pleases."[33] Black said that children often were not mature enough to judge when and where protests were appropriate, and that students were not likely "wise enough, even with

Justice Abe Fortas wrote the majority opinion for the *Tinker* case, declaring that students do not "shed their constitutional rights . . . at the schoolhouse gate."

this Court's expert help from Washington, to run the 23,390 public school systems in our 50 states."[34]

In 1992, in Des Moines, John and Mary Beth Tinker and Christopher Eckhardt met with alumni and high school students to reflect on the case. Eckhardt recalled thinking that the Supreme Court decision marked "a proud day in America for the First Amendment."[35] Dick Moberly, a math teacher during the late 1960s, later said that he would tell young people this: "You have a right to express

96

Justice Hugo Black wrote a dissenting opinion for the *Tinker* case, arguing that students are not mature enough to decide when and where political protests are appropriate.

your opinion but no right to belittle or degrade people publicly. I want freedom of speech with responsibility. How to curb it to protect innocent people is difficult."[36]

Many issues arise in cases like these. Should schools ban talk about controversial current events or very emotional topics? Should all symbols be banned if some are banned? Should school officials try to prevent disorder or must they wait until it occurs? Should students be allowed to wear a swastika, symbol of Nazi Germany and its hatred of Jews, in a class where teachers or students are Jewish? Ku Klux Klan symbols in a school with African Americans? These acts are not violent and could be called "silent expression," but with grave consequences. Opponents might find these forms of expression too troublesome to be allowed.

Issues of Personal Appearance

In 1989, about one hundred students in Henry County, Georgia, picketed the superintendent's office. Sixty boys had been suspended from school because their hair touched their collars, violating the dress code. Other schools have similar policies. In Jaspar, Alabama, a parent complained to the school board when her son, a sophomore, was suspended for hair that was one inch too long. She called the rule "an invasion of privacy," and said, "His hair doesn't have anything to do with his education."[37]

A thirteen-year-old in Milford, Connecticut, was sent home for coming to school with pink hair. She and her mother disputed the school's right to suspend her unless she wore a wig or changed her hair back to its normal shade. They said it restricted her freedom of expression. The school rule prohibited "costume style makeup or hair colorings" and aimed to prevent disruptions in school.[38] The student said, "I'm not hurting anyone. I'm not harassing anyone. This is my personal conviction. It's a pinkish red color I like very much. . . . This is not a costume. This is the way I live."[39]

Besides hair, schools have regulated other aspects of personal appearance. In 1993, schools in Broward County, Florida, prohibited wearing undergarments as outer clothing. In Illinois in 1986, the Wills County school district banned clothing it labelled "promiscuous" and clothing with profanity printed on either side. Students must also wear socks with shoes or sandals.

Gary Marx, a spokesman for the American Association

of School Administrators comments, "We do see indications here and there that schools are thinking about dress codes and how students are attired may affect their education and the education of others."[40] The American Civil Liberties Union's position on students' grooming and hairstyles is that these things should not concern officials unless they disrupt education or threaten safety.[41]

Some dress codes aim to protect students. For example, schools in Syracuse, New York, and Los Angeles, California, have banned clothing that signifies gang membership. Some high schools across the country ban extremely expensive clothing, jewelry, and other costly items for fear of fights or theft.[42] In 1996, President Bill Clinton spoke in favor of school uniforms as a way to improve discipline and reduce crime.

To downplay appearance issues, some public schools have adopted uniforms, which also save families money. A New Orleans school spokesperson said uniforms are also "a security issue" since when students wear uniforms, it's easy to recognize outsiders.[43] Yet some students and others protest that such rules violate their right to free expression. The United States Supreme Court has not dealt directly with the issue and lower courts have issued opinions both for and against the codes.

8

An Ongoing Debate

Issues regarding what students can say, hear, and read are heating up in new areas. Nonprint media—TV, music videos, videotape, film, radio, compact disk, hypertext for personal computers—are increasingly used by young people. According to the National Council of Teachers of English (NCTE), these are becoming "primary sources of information and recreation, as well as emotional and artistic experiences for Americans."[1] The NCTE says that in order to help students learn how to identify stereotyping, propaganda, and other devices used to persuade audiences, teachers might need to expose students to controversial materials and discuss them.[2]

The NCTE notes that teachers may omit these materials from classroom study out of fear of conflict and censorship. There is also direct censorship when teachers are told "[not to] show any film or videotape rated

'R'—ratings which our courts have called irrelevant for instructional purposes. . . . "[3] The NCTE believes that students should learn more about all kinds of media in order to make informed decisions in a media-saturated society.

As technology expands, the cyberspace frontier brings more people in touch with each other and with written material. America Online, a computer information service, has already banned or censored certain groups and individuals for the content of their messages on networks and in discussion forums—for example, by banning racist messages.

Messages sent on computers through student bulletin boards have led to controversial legal cases. In 1994, some male students at Santa Rosa Junior College in California posted sexual comments about a female student on the computer bulletin board run by the university. Students could choose to use the board or not.

Three female students complained to the United States Department of Education Office for Civil Rights that sex discrimination had occurred. The office ruled that one of the female students had been subjected to sexual harassment: a hostile educational atmosphere at the college newspaper where she worked with three men who had posted messages about her. The women who had complained agreed to settle their cases with the college, who paid them each fifteen thousand dollars.

Author Anthony Lewis expressed strong concerns that the federal government would be involved in such a case and that the college had to face this kind of legal problem. Saying that "the students should learn about free speech," Lewis went on, "genuine sexual harassment is an outrage. But claims of insensitive words should not be allowed to override the First Amendment, least of all in the free atmosphere of a university."[4]

Others also disagreed with the outcome of this case. Attorney and author Michael Godwin said:

> If freedom of speech means anything, it means the ability to express your anger or frustration with another person. And freedom of association means you get to choose who you talk to. Here we have a case where guys are talking to each other, saying some obnoxious and hateful things, but deliberately avoiding saying them to the women. What should have happened is that people who objected to the content should have called the guy who posted the message a jerk.[5]

In another case, a University of Florida student was banned from using the school's computer network after posting repeated messages with political arguments. In 1989, officials at Stanford University in California banned a Usenet discussion group after someone inserted a joke viewed as being anti-Semitic. Stanford later changed its mind after being accused of censorship.

The Office for Civil Rights proposed a ban on computer bulletin board comments that harass, denigrate, or show hostility toward a person or group based on sex, race, or color, including slurs, negative stereotypes, jokes, or pranks.

Many schools are already hooked up to the Internet, a web of computer networks designed by Defense Department contractors during the 1960s to withstand nuclear war. As a result, the battle over educational materials may escalate, since many books and ideas students would not find in school libraries are available through the Internet. There are very controversial materials, including guides on how to commit acts that most people find criminal or appalling. According to Stephen Bates, "Schools can keep a pornographic book off the library shelf by not buying it, but they can't keep it from entering the building through cyberspace. Limiting a user's access to material on it is nearly impossible."[6] Libby Black, director of the Boulder Valley School District's Internet Project in Colorado, has said that when schools consider whether to make the use of the Internet available to students, "the situation is essentially all or nothing."[7]

Groups that oppose censorship have noted the complexity of cyberspace communication. Leslie Harris, director of public policy for People For the American Way (PAW), has said that although PAW usually thinks library books should not be kept from young people, pornographic images and certain other materials found on the Internet "may require a different answer."[8]

What are schools doing? Some supervise students closely and enforce strict rules regarding computers. Students may go on-line only for specific purposes. Many schools also require students to fill out forms describing each on-line session. Some must even log onto their Internet accounts with "smartcards" that record their on-line movements. They may also need signed parental permission forms for certain activities.[9] Schools express special concern about illegal or sexually oriented material. Some rules ban students from using the computer to send abusive E-mail messages.

Computer engineers are developing technical solutions

to these problems, such as ways to keep certain users from going beyond given zones on the Internet. Educators who believe that students should learn to use the Internet hope that schools will not lose the opportunity to provide that experience.

Asked for their opinions on this issue late in 1994, three major conservative groups said that they had not yet fully studied the subject of Internet access in public schools. In the meantime, in the summer of 1995, the Senate passed an amendment to the telecommunications bill, making it a crime to spread certain sexual material on the Internet. The vote was 84 to 16. Among those who had reservations about the bill was Senator Patrick Leahy. Leahy had proposed an alternative bill that he felt would "accomplish the goal of keeping pornography away from children without imposing a new layer of government censorship and without destroying the Internet."[10]

The debate over cyberspace and the schools will no doubt continue. Like other conflicts over censorship, it is not easy to resolve.

Increasing Public Awareness

Anticensorship groups want the public to learn more about censorship. Each September, many libraries hold a Banned Books Week. They exhibit books that have been targets of censorship and urge citizens to think about the issues of free expression and the right to read. Some libraries also invite authors to share their personal experiences with censorship. The American Library Association encourages these efforts. Opponents of censorship point out the dangers. Author Edward Jenkinson warns, "Freedom of speech, freedom to read,

A display during Banned Books Week at a Connecticut high school.

the right to know, and the right to teach are among the very first targets of totalitarian societies."[11]   Other organizations also inform the public about censorship. During the 1980s, the Library of Congress's Center for the Book began supporting efforts by booksellers and by the National Coalition Against Censorship to post lists of banned books in bookstores and to provide films about censorship to TV stations.

In 1995, the Mark Twain Memorial House in Hartford, Connecticut, sponsored workshops for teachers. Teachers were shown how to help students understand how Twain used irony in *Huckleberry Finn* to reveal the racism and hypocrisy of society during that era.

Competing Views and Values

At the heart of many censorship conflicts are differing views about the purpose of the public education system. Expressing a point of view that rejects censorship, Timothy Dyk says:

> America was rooted in a desire to create a common educational experience for the wave of immigrants which came to this country in the late 19th and early 20th centuries. Public education not only taught immigrant students to read and write the English language, it educated them about the political life of the United States, exposed them to individuals with a different heritage and exposed the existing American population to the diverse viewpoints of its new arrivals . . . Today . . . the system still rests on a commitment to create politically aware, thoughtful and responsible citizens and to instill tolerance for diversity by exposing students to a wide variety of views.[12]

Jocelyn Chadwick-Joshua lectures at the 1995 Mark Twain House Summer Teacher's Institute.

In 1989, John Buchanan, a Baptist minister and chairman of People For the American Way, said, "We are witnessing in these skirmishes the clash of two competing views of public education in America. The censors see efforts to teach our children about the world around them as a threat; the rest of us see it as a way to broaden our children's vistas and opportunities."[13] Buchanan contends, "Most parents want schools that promote tolerance and pluralism and teach children to think critically and behave responsibly. He urges people to "support the freedom to learn."[14]

Other, more personal fears affect the debate. Editor and publisher Richard W. Jackson, who worked with Judy Blume, said:

> Through her books, Judy says, "It's your life. How are you going to live it?" That question is very troublesome to [people] who don't want their kids to think for themselves. Their desire to have complete control over their children is an outgrowth of the panic they must feel when confronted with the realities of modern times.[15]

When conflicts involve deeply held values and views about the education of children, emotions can run high. Open public discussions will allow different viewpoints to be expressed and defended. More participation by more people will ensure that no single person or group determines what all others learn.

Students can become involved, too. Young people have been involved in many famous censorship cases, taking a stand and expressing their different opinions. Perhaps your community or school library takes part in Banned Books Week or other related activities? You

John Buchanan, the former chair of People For the American Way, contends that allowing students to have access to various materials may broaden their perspectives.

might ask the librarians and teachers about their experiences with censorship. They may have had to make difficult decisions about books or other materials or programs. You may also want to know what procedures your school has to handle complaints.

As you continue your education and consider what you are learning and how, you may develop your own answers to these questions: What should students see, hear, read, or say? What may teachers teach? Who should decide? These questions affect the students and educators of today and will continue to affect new generations of Americans.

The Ten Most Frequently Attacked Books

(1982–1994)

1. *Of Mice and Men* (John Steinbeck)
2. *The Catcher in the Rye* (J. D. Salinger)
3. *The Chocolate War* (Robert Cormier)
4. *Scary Stories to Tell in the Dark* (Alvin Schwartz)
5. *The Adventures of Huckleberry Finn* (Mark Twain)
6. *Go Ask Alice* (Anonymous)
7. *I Know Why the Caged Bird Sings* (Maya Angelou)
8. *The Witches* (Roald Dahl)
9. *Bridge to Terabithia* (Katherine Paterson)
10. *A Light in the Attic* (Shel Silverstein)

Source: *People For the American Way*

Organizations to Contact

American Association of School Administrators
1801 North Moore St.
Arlington, VA 22209
(703) 528-0700

American Civil Liberties Union (ACLU)
132 West 43rd St.
New York, NY 10036
(212) 944-9800

American Library Association
50 East Huron St.
Chicago, IL 60611
(312) 944-6780

Office for Intellectual Freedom and Freedom to Read Foundation work to defend intellectual freedom. Publishes pamphlets, books, audiovisual aids and a bibliography called "Pressure Groups and Censorship."

Americans United For Separation of Church and State
1816 Jefferson Pl., NW
Washington, DC 20036
(202) 466-3234

Nonprofit group that researches religious liberty education. Distributes pamphlets including "The Equal Access Act and Public Schools" and "Religion in the Public Schools Curriculum."

National Coalition Against Censorship
275 7th Ave., 20th Floor
New York, NY 10001
(212) 807-6222

An alliance of groups that work to defend the freedom of expression. Public education and advocacy. The NCAC's publications include "Censorship News" and "Report on Book Censorship Litigation in Public Schools."

National Council of Teachers of English
1111 West Kenyon Rd.
Urbana, IL 61801-1096
(217) 328-3870 ext. 283
(800) 369-6283

Operates SLATE (Support for Learning and Teaching of English), its official intellectual freedom network. Distributes a pamphlet called "The Students' Right to Read," sometimes used as a model for handling censorship complaints, and published "Guidelines for Dealing with Censorship of Nonprint Materials." Materials on challenged books and support in dealing with challenges.

National Education Association
1201 16th St., NW
Washington, DC, 20036
(202) 833-4000

National Organization on Legal Problems in Education
Southwest Plaza, Suite 223
3061 Southwest 29th St.
Topeka, KS 66614
(913) 273-3550

Office for Intellectual Freedom
American Library Association
50 East Huron St.
Chicago, IL 60611
(312) 944-6780

Parents' Music Resource Center (PMRC)
1500 Arlington Blvd., Suite 300
Arlington, VA 22209
(703) 527-9466

People For the American Way
2000 M St., NW, Suite 400
Washington, DC 20036
(202) 467-4999

Student Press Law Center
1101 Wilson Blvd., Suite 1910
Arlington, VA 22209
(703) 807-1904

Chapter Notes

Chapter 1

1. *Attacks On the Freedom to Learn, 1993–94 Report,* People For the American Way, Washington, D.C., p. 178.

2. Quoted in Charles Suhor, "The New Censors: Assaults from the Right and the Left," *Forum,* November/December 1992, p. 8.

3. Quoted in Linda Greenhouse, "High Court Limits Banning of Books," *The New York Times,* June 26, 1982, p. A10.

4. Quoted in "The Island Trees Case Turns Another Legal Corner," *The New York Times,* June 27, 1982, Section 4, p. 8.

5. Edward B. Jenkinson, *Censors in the Classroom: The Mind Benders* (Carbondale, Ill.: Southern Illinois University Press, 1979), pp. 124–125.

Chapter 2

1. Lee Burress, *Battle of the Books: Literary Censorship in the Public Schools, 1950–1985* (Metuchen, N.J.: The Scarecrow Press, Inc., 1989), p. 9.

2. *Funk and Wagnall's New Encyclopedia,* eds. Leon L. Bram and Norma H. Dickey (New York: Rand McNally, 1986), vol. 5, p. 411.

3. Burress, p. 9.

4. Ibid., pp. 99–100.

5. Ibid., p. 9.

6. National Coalition Against Censorship, *Fighting the Religious Right in Schools,* National Coalition Against Censorship, New York.

7. Edward B. Jenkinson, *Censors in the Classroom: The Mind Benders* (Carbondale, Ill.: Southern Illinois University Press, 1979), p. 113.

8. American Library Association, *Banned Books* (Chicago: American Library Association, 1995), p. 4.

9. Quoted in Jenkinson, p. 138.

10. Quoted in Gary Wireman, "Town Torn Over School Program," *The Charlotte Observer*, April 4, 1993, p. 8A.

11. *Attacks On the Freedom to Learn, 1993–94 Report*, People For the American Way, Washington, D.C., p. 14.

12. Ibid.

13. Ibid.

14. National Council of Teachers of English, *The Students' Right to Read*, National Council of Teachers of English, Chicago, Ill., 1962, p. 1.

15. Bill Graves, "The Pressure Group Cooker," *The School Administrator*, April 1992, p. 9.

16. Gary Wireman, "Town Torn Over School Program," *Charlotte Observer*, April 4, 1993, p. 8A.

17. *Attacks On the Freedom to Learn*, p. 5.

18. Jenkinson, p. xix.

19. Lester Asheim, "Not Censorship But Selection," *Wilson Library Bulletin*, September 1953, p. 67.

20. *School Censorship: Questions and Answers*, People For the American Way, Washington, D.C.

21. Joseph E. Bryson and Elizabeth W. Detty, *Censorship of Public School Library and Instructional Material* (Charlottesville, Va.: The Michie Company, 1982), p. 10.

22. Quoted in Jenkinson, p. 137.

23. Quoted in People For the American Way, *Forum*, Winter 1990, p. 2.

24. Ibid.

25. Quoted in Bradley Steffens, *Free Speech: Identifying Propaganda Techniques* (San Diego, Calif.: Greenhaven Press, 1992), p. 23.

Chapter 3

1. From *The New England Courant*, quoted in Carl Van Doren, *Benjamin Franklin* (New York: Viking, 1938), pp. 27–28.

2. Brandt Aymar and Edward Sagarin, *A Pictorial History of the World's Greatest Trials* (New York: Bonanza Books, 1967), p. 101.

3. Ibid., p. 106.

4. Ibid., p. 105.

5. See Robert S. Alley, ed., *James Madison on Religious Liberty* (Buffalo, N.Y.: Prometheus Press, 1985), p 19.

6. *Funk and Wagnall's New Encyclopedia*, eds. Leon L. Bram and Norma H. Dickey (New York: Rand McNally, 1986), vol. 5, p. 415.

7. *Schenck* v. *United States*, 249 U.S. 47, 1919, 39 S. Ct. 247, L. Ed. 2d.

8. Todd S. Purdam, "President Defends a Place for Religion in the Schools," *The New York Times*, July 13, 1995, pp. A1, B10. See also: Fred W. Friendly and Martha J. H. Elliot, *The Constitution: That Delicate Balance* (New York: Random House, 1984).

9. George Sullivan, *The Day Women Got the Vote* (New York: Scholastic, 1994), pp. 14–15.

10. *Evans* v. *Shelma Union High School District of Fresno County*, 222 P. 801 (Ca. 1924).

11. National Council of Teachers of English, *The Students' Right to Read*, National Council of Teachers of English, Chicago, Ill., 1962, p. 1.

12. Quoted in Bill Graves, "The Pressure Group Cooker," *The School Administrator*, April 1992, p. 12.

13. Quoted in Onalee McGraw, *Secular Humanism and the Schools: The Issue Whose Time Has Come* (a monograph published by The Heritage Foundation in: *Education Update*, September 1977), p. 17.

14. *Human Values in Children's Books*, The Council on Interracial Books for Children.

15. Ibid.

16. *The Students' Right to Read*, p. 1.

Chapter 4

1. Jonathan Rabinowitz, "'Huckleberry Finn' Without Fear," *The New York Times*, July 23, 1995, Section 13 (*Connecticut Weekly*), p. 1.

2. Joan DelFattore, *What Johnny Shouldn't Read: Textbook Censorship in America* (New Haven, Conn.: Yale University Press, 1992), p. 132.

3. "Ban the Books, Fire the Teachers," *Censorship News*, Issue 2, 1995, No. 58, p. 1.

4. Quoted in "The Censor in the Rye," *Forum*, People For the American Way, Winter 1990, p. 8.

5. Nat Hentoff, *The First Freedom: The Tumultuous History of Free Speech in America* (New York: Delacorte Press, 1980), pp. 27–28.

6. As quoted in Mark I. West, *Trust Your Children: Voices Against Censorship in Children's Literature* (New York: Neal-Schuman Publishers, 1988), p. 35.

7. Ibid.

8. DelFattore, pp. 129-133.

9. American Library Association, *Banned Books* (Chicago, Ill.: ALA, 1995), p. 4.

10. Merideth Tax, "Yes in Virginia, Too," *The New York Times*, March 18, 1994, p. A28.

11. *Banned Books*, p. 20.

12. Ibid., p. 18.

13. Ibid., p. 38.

14. Ibid., p. 46.

15. Lee Burress, *Battle of the Books: Literary Censorship in the Public Schools, 1950–1985* (Metuchen, N.J.: The Scarecrow Press, Inc., 1989), p. 100.

16. Ibid., p. 178.

17. Ibid., p. 119.

18. Ibid., p. 128.

19. Ibid., pp. 123–124.

20. *Newsletter on Intellectual Freedom*, American Library Association, January 1979, p. 5.

21. Quoted in Hentoff, p. 24.

22. Ibid., p. 25.

23. *Banned Books*, p. 146.

24. *Todd* v. *Rochester Community Schools*, 200 N. W. 2d. 90 (Mich. App. 1972).

25. *President's Council, District 25* v. *Community School Board No. 25*, 457 F. 2d Cir. 1972, 409 U.S. 999–1000 (1972).

26. Quoted in Hentoff, pp. 35–36.

27. *Right to Read Defense Committee* v. *School Committee of the City of Chelsea*, 454 F. Supp. 703 D. Mass. (1978), in *Banned Books*, p. 84.

28. *Minarcini* v. *Strongsville City School District*, 384 F. Supp. 698, aff'd, 541. F. 2d 577 (6th Cir. 1976) p. 581.

29. DelFattore, p. 109.

30. Letter to the Editor, *Panama City News Herald*, May 14, 1987.

31. DelFattore, pp. 109-110.

32. *Board of Education, Island Trees School Union Free School District No. 26* v. *Pico*, 457 U.S. 853, 102 Sup. Ct. 2799, (1982).

33. *Banned Books*, p. 63.

34. Quoted in Burress, p. 151.

35. Ibid.

36. Ibid., p. 11.

37. Ibid.

38. Ken Donelson, "Ten Steps Toward the Freedom to Read," *The ALAN Review*, Winter 1993, Vol. 20, No. 2, p. 15.

39. Ibid., p. 15.

40. Ibid., p. 17.

41. Ibid., pp. 18–19.

Chapter 5

1. Quoted in Nat Hentoff, *The First Freedom: The Tumultuous History of Free Speech in America* (New York: Delacorte Press, 1980), p. 41.

2. Ibid.

3. *Attacks On the Freedom to Learn, 1993–94 Report,* People For the American Way, Washington, D.C., p. 15.

4. *Knarr* v. *Board of School Trustees,* in Hentoff, p. 42.

5. *Sterzing* v. *Fort Bend Independent School District,* 376 F. Dupp. 657 (1972).

6. Hentoff, pp. 47–48.

7. Quoted in Hentoff, p. 50.

8. Ibid., p. 53.

9. Ibid.

10. "Montana School Board Learns Costs of Censorship," *Newsletter,* ACLU Arts Censorship Project, Spring 1995, pp. 1, 6.

11. "Teaching Self-Image Stirs Furor," *The New York Times,* October 13, 1993, p. B6.

12. Ibid.

13. Ibid.

14. Ibid.

15. Ibid.

16. Quoted in Edward Jenkinson, "Writing Assignments, Journals, and Student Privacy," *ERIC Digest,* (Bloomington, Ind.: Indiana University, 1993), p. 1.

17. Roz Udow, "Censorship: An Elitist Weapon," *SIECUS Report, July 1985,* p. 2.

18. Jenkinson, p. 2.

19. Robert Emmet Long, ed., *Censorship* (New York: H.W. Wilson, 1990), pp. 144–146.

20. Udow, p. 3.

21. Bill Graves, "The Pressure Group Cooker," *The School Administrator,* April 1992, p. 10.

22. Quoted in Stephen Bates, "A Textbook of Virtues," *The New York Times Education Life*, January 8, 1995, p. A4.

23. Ibid.

24. Quoted in Sonia L. Nazario, "Crusader Vows to Put God Back Into Schools Using Local Elections," *The Wall Street Journal*, July 15, 1993, p. 1.

25. Ibid.

26. Stephen R. Goldstein, "The Asserted Constitutional Right of Public School Teachers to Determine What They Teach," *University of Pennsylvania Law Review*, June 1976, 124, pp. 1293–1357.

27. *Bob Cary et. al.* v. *Board of Education for the Adams-Arapahoe School District 28-J Aurora, Colorado*, 427 F. Supp. 945, 952 (D. Colo. 1977), pp. 15–16. (Case reversed on appeal.)

28. Butler Act, quoted in Tom McGowen, *The Great Monkey Trial: Science Versus Fundamentalism in America* (New York: Franklin Watts, 1990), p. 31.

29. McGowen, p. 72.

30. Arthur Blake, *The Scopes Trial: Defending the Right to Teach* (Brookfield, Conn.: The Millbrook Press, 1994), p. 29.

31. McGowen, p. 58.

32. Ibid., p. 64.

33. Blake, p. 50.

34. *Epperson* v. *Arkansas*, 393 U.S. 97 (1968).

35. *McClean* v. *Arkansas Board of Education*, 663 F. 2d 47 8th Cir. (1981).

36. Brief filed in *Edwards* v. *Aguillard*, 107 S. Ct. 2573 (1987).; in Peter Irons, *The Courage of Their Convictions* (New York: The Free Press, 1988), p. 217.

37. Ibid.

38. Joan DelFattore, *What Johnny Shouldn't Read: Textbook Censorship in America* (New Haven, Conn.: Yale University Press, 1992), p. 135.

39. Quoted in McGowen, p. 12.

40. Blake, p. 60.

Chapter 6

1. Bill Graves, "The Pressure Group Cooker," *The School Administrator*, April 1992, p. 8.

2. Ibid., p. 9.

3. Joan DelFattore, *What Johnny Shouldn't Read: Textbook Censorship in America* (New Haven, Conn.: Yale University Press, 1992), p. 5.

4. Ibid., pp. 4–5.

5. Quoted in "See Jim and Pat Cook. Jim Cooks First," *The New York Times*, March 13, 1986, p. A26.

6. Ibid.

7. Ibid.

8. *Mozert* v. *Hawkins County Board of Education*, 827 F2d. 1058 (6th Cir. 1987).

9. Ray Bradbury, in Coda to *Fahrenheit 451* (Cutchogue, N.Y.: Buccaneer Books, 1994), p. 177.

10. Ibid.

11. "California's Bill Honig Moves Against the Censors of U.S. Textbooks," *People*, October 11, 1985, pp. 57–63.

12. DelFattore, pp. 145–146.

13. Ibid., p. 157.

14. Quoted in Paul Weingarten, "Texas Takes on E-word in Schools," *Chicago Tribune*, February 13, 1989, Section 1, p. 5.

15. Quoted in DelFattore, p. 164.

16. Robert Rotham, "Both Sides Claim a Victory in Texas Evolution Vote," *Education Week*, March 22, 1989, p. 1.

17. In its Report of the Commissioner of Education Concerning Recommended Changes and Corrections in Textbooks, 1990, p. 74.

18. *Newsletter on Intellectual Freedom*, NCTE, March 1977, p. 46.

19. DelFattore, p. 148.

20. Ibid., p. 9.

Chapter 7

1. Quoted in Nat Hentoff, *The First Freedom: The Tumultuous History of Free Speech in America* (New York: Delacorte Press, 1980), p. 11.

2. Ibid., p. 13.

3. *Dickey* v. *Alabama State Board of Education*, in Jules Archer, *You and the Law* (New York: Harcourt, 1978), p. 50.

4. Archer, p. 50.

5. Quoted in Hentoff, pp. 15–16.

6. *Newsletter*, ACLU Arts Censorship Project, Fall-Winter 1994, p. 4.

7. Quoted in Hentoff, p. 15.

8. Quoted in Edmund Lindop, *The Bill of Rights and Landmark Cases* (New York: Franklin Watts, 1989), p. 135.

9. Quoted in Lindop, p. 136.

10. Ibid. (*Hazelwood* v. *St. Louis Independent School District*, S. Ct. 1988).

11. Lindop, p. 5.

12. Ibid., p. 7.

13. Sam and Beryl Epstein, *Kids In Court: The ACLU Defends Their Rights* (New York: Four Winds Press, 1984), p. 153.

14. Ibid., p. 160.

15. Hentoff, p. 14.

16. *Bethel School District* v. *Matthew Fraser*, S. Ct. 1986.

17. Quoted in Dr. Archie Loss, "Censorship in the 'Nineties,'" *Journal of the Northwestern Pennsylvania Council of Teachers of English*, Winter 1992, pp. 6–7.

18. "The First Amendment, Under Fire From the Left: Whose Free Speech?," Moderated by Anthony Lewis, *The New York Times Sunday Magazine*, May 13, 1994, p. 43.

19. Anthony Lewis, "Time to Grow Up," *The New York Times*, October 14, 1994, p. A35.

20. Franklyn G. Jenifer, "Hate Speech Is Still Free Speech," *The New York Times*, May 13, 1994, p. A31.

21. "The First Amendment, Under Fire From the Left," p. 42.

22. Ibid., p. 43.

23. Ibid.

24. Ibid., p. 44.

25. *West Virginia State Board of Education* v. *Barnette*, 319 U.S. 624 (1943), in Anson Phelps Stokes and Leo Pfeffer, *Church and State in the United States* (New York: Harper and Row, 1964), pp. 124–125.

26. Hentoff, pp. 180–181.

27. Ibid., p. 183.

28. *Blackwell* v. *Issaquena County Board of Education*, F. 2nd 749 (1966).

29. *Adderly* v. *State of Florida*, 385 U.S. 39 (1966).

30. Hentoff, pp. 3–4.

31. Quoted in Hentoff, p. 5.

32. Doreen Rappaport, *Tinker vs. Des Moines: Student Rights on Trial* (New York: HarperCollins, 1993), p. 130.

33. Epstein, p. 46.

34. Ibid., p. 41.

35. Quoted in Rappaport, p. 134.

36. Ibid., p. 139.

37. "Crosscurrents on Dress in High Schools," *The New York Times*, September 13, 1989, p. B10.

38. "Pink Hair Day Prompts Dispute," *The New York Times*, September 2, 1994, p. B4.

39. Ibid.

40. Quoted in "Crosscurrents on Dress in High Schools," p. B10.

41. "Pink Hair Day Prompts Dispute," p. B4.

42. "You Cannot Play This or Wear That," *The New York Times*, April 9, 1995, p. E2.

43. "Crosscurrents on Dress in High Schools," p. B10.

Chapter 8

1. NCTE Task Force, *Guidelines for Dealing With Censorship Of Nonprint Materials*, NCTE: Urbana, Ill., p. 2.

2. Ibid., pp. 2–3.

3. Ibid., p. 3.

4. Anthony Lewis, "Time to Grow Up," *The New York Times*, October 14, 1994, p. A35.

5. Tamar Lewin, "Dispute Over Computer Messages: Free Speech or Sexual Harassment?" *The New York Times*, September 22, 1994, p. D22.

6. Stephen Bates, "The Next Front in the Book Wars," *The New York Times Education Life Magazine*, November 6, 1994, p. 22.

7. Quoted in Bates, p. 22.

8. Ibid., p. 23.

9. Bates, p. 22.

10. Quoted in "Senate Caves In, Passes Internet Smut Bill," *Censorship News*, Issue 2, No. 58, 1995, p. 3.

11. Edward B. Jenkinson, *Censors in the Classroom: The Mind Benders* (Carbondale, Ill.: Southern Illinois University Press, 1979), p. 163.

12. Timothy Dyk, "Textbook Ruling Creates Dilemma," *Bristol Herald-Courier*, December 15, 1986, Op-ed; reprinted in *Press Clips*, People For the American Way, January–March 1987, p. 18.

13. Quoted in Muriel Cohen, "Study Finds Rise in Attacks on Books, Sex-ed," *The Boston Globe*, August 31, 1989, reprinted in *Press Clips*, Fall 1989, p. 9.

14. John N. Buchanan, "Censorship Lives in Public Schools," *The South Dade News Leader*, October 26, 1988, Op-ed.

15. Mark I. West, *Trust Your Children: Voices Against Censorship in Children's Literature* (New York: Neal-Schuman, 1988), p. 106.

Further Reading

Atkinson, Linda. *Your Legal Rights.* New York: Franklin Watts, 1982.

Bernstein, Richard B., and Jerome Agel. *Into the Third Century: The Supreme Court.* New York: Walker, 1989.

Brown, Jean, ed. *Preserving Intellectual Freedom: Fighting Censorship in Our Schools.* Urbana, Ill.: National Council of Teachers of English, 1994.

Donelson, Kenneth, ed. *The Students' Right to Read.* Urbana, Ill.: National Council of Teachers of English, 1972.

Downs, Robert B. and Ralph E. McCoy, eds. *The First Freedom Today: Critical Essays Relating to Censorship and to Intellectual Freedom.* Chicago: American Library Association, 1984.

Faber, Doris, and Harold Faber. *We the People: The Story of the Constitution Since 1787.* New York: Scribners, 1987.

Friendly, Fred. *The Constitution: That Delicate Balance.* New York: Random House, 1984.

Fulwiler, Toby. *Guidelines for Using Journals in School Settings.* Urbana Ill. National Council of Teachers of English, 1987.

Graff, Gerald. *Beyond the Culture Wars: How Teaching the Conflicts Can Revitalize American Education.* New York: W.W. Norton, 1992.

Green, Jonathon. *The Encyclopedia of Censorship.* New York: Facts On File, 1990.

Gregorian, Vartan. *Censorship: Five Hundred Years of Conflict.* New York: Oxford University Press, 1984.

Hill, Samuel S., and Dennis E. Owen. *The New Religious Political Right.* Nashville, Tenn.: Abingdon, 1982.

Horn, Carl, ed. *Whose Values? The Battle for Morality in Pluralistic America.* Ann Arbor, Mich.: Servant Books, 1985.

Lawson, Don. *Landmark Supreme Court Cases.* Hillside, N.J.: Enslow Publishers, Inc., 1987.

Levine, Alan H. and Eve Cary. *Rights of Students.* New York: Avon, 1977.

Meltzer, Milton. *The Bill of Rights: How We Got It and What It Means.* New York: Thomas Y. Crowell, 1990.

Monroe, Judy. *Censorship.* New York: Crestwood House, 1990.

O'Neil, Robert M. *Classrooms in the Crossfire: The Rights and Interests of Students, Parents, Teachers, Administrators, Librarians, and the Community.* Bloomington, Ind.: Indiana University Press, 1981.

Rappaport, Doreen. *Be the Judge, Be the Jury: Hazelwood vs. St. Louis Independent School District.* New York: HarperCollins, 1994.

————. *Be the Judge, Be the Jury: Pico vs. Island Trees Long Island School District.* New York: HarperCollins, 1995.

Steffens, Bradley. *Free Speech: Identifying Propaganda Techniques.* San Diego: Greenhaven Press, 1992.

Zeinert, Karen. *Free Speech: From Newspapers to Music Lyrics.* Springfield, N.J.: Enslow Publishers, Inc., 1995.

Index